The Milkweed Ladies

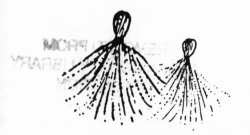

The Milkweed Ladies

Louise McNeill

University of Pittsburgh Press

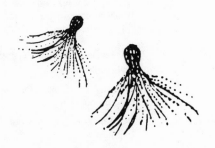

Published by the University of Pittsburgh Press,
Pittsburgh, Pa., 15260
Copyright © 1988, University of Pittsburgh Press
All rights reserved
Feffer and Simons, Inc., London
Manufactured in the United States of America

Library of Congress Cataloging-in-Publication Data

McNeill, Louise.
    The milkweed ladies.

    1. McNeill, Louise—Biography—Youth. 2. Poets,
American—20th century—Biography. 3. Farm life—
West Virginia. 4. West Virginia—Social life and
customs. I. Title.
PS3525.A283Z467 1988   811'.52 [B]   88-1334
ISBN 0-8229-3587-2
ISBN 0-8229-5406-0 (pbk.)

A portion of this book first appeared in *Appalachian Review*,
vol. 13, no. 4, 1985.

"Night at the Commodore" first appeared in *Northwest Review*,
vol. 22, nos. 1–2, 1984.

My thanks to the editors of these journals for permission to
reprint.

To Roger W. Pease
whose earth-love and long labor
went into the slow construction
of this book

THE RIVER

Now they have bridged the canyon of the Gauley
And built a lock above the Swago shoal
To float the barges past the lazy shallow
With loads of river sand and mountain coal.

Along the shore where passing Mingo warriors
Built drift-wood fires to parch Ohio maize
Cook ovens glare red-eyed upon the darkness
And belch their cinders at the fevered days.

But in the broken rushes of the inlet
Where herons rose with beaten-winged alarm
That autumn evening when an Irish rascal
Knelt by the stream to bathe his wounded arm,
. . . White herons sleep, their folded wings unstained
By all that blood the savage Gauley drained
From pale-faced men whose kindred now possess
The last dark current of the wilderness.

—from *Gauley Mountain*
(New York: Harcourt Brace, 1939)

Contents

Acknowledgments   *xi*

A Patch of Earth   *3*

G.D.'s Sea Chest   *9*

Granny Fanny's Thorn Broom Handle   *17*

The Door Peg   *31*

Green-up Time   *41*

Apple Butter Red   *57*

Neighborhood Ways   *65*

Signs and Portents   *81*

Over Bonnie   *93*

The Coming of the Roads   *103*

Night at the Commodore   *115*

Acknowledgments

Acknowledgment and appreciation to staff mem-bers of the University of Pittsburgh Press: Frederick A. Hetzel, Catherine Marshall, and Peter Oresick.

My gratitude to Maggie Anderson, a young poet from West Virginia. Maggie believed in *The Milkweed Ladies* and, when I was disabled by an accident, volunteered to act as my agent. She was successful in placing the book, and then gave her editorial skill, her poetic intuition, and her knowledge of the mountain culture as she and I shaped and tightened the manuscript to its final form.

Many others have contributed editorial suggestions, financial aid, encouragement, and factual notes. My appreciation to Norman Fagan, René de Chochor, Walter Havighurst, Ruth Cantor, Dr. Robert Munn (deceased), Gayle Mason, Sharon Tate, Larry Groce, Thelma D. Quick, "Young Jim," Annabelle, Rae, Doug, "J.B.," Devon, Jean, and Reed W.

Among those who, in the period 1865–1988, saved or helped to save "The Farm": Captain Jim and Granny; G.D. and Grace; Jim and Annabelle. Also Ward K., in his time; "C.P.," in his time; The Slashing, in its year; and—in current time—Elisabeth, Blix, Cheryl, Doug and Dave Morrison, and Jamie C.

Milkweed ladies, so fair and fine,

Won't you have a sip of my columbine?

Or a thimble of thimbleberry wine?

A Patch of Earth

*T*he farm, *a wide plateau of rocky, loam-*
dark fields, lies above Swago Crick, along
the Greenbrier River of West Virginia and
some twenty-five to thirty miles north of
the Virginia line. This patch of earth is
held within a half stadium of limestone
cliffs and mountain pastures. On the surface, the Swago Farm is quiet and solid,
green in summer and in winter deep with
snow. It has its level fields, its fence rows
and hilly pastures. There are some two hundred acres of trees and bluegrass, running
water, and the winding, dusty paths that
cattle and humans have kept open through
the years. There are three small woodlands,
two of them still virgin and mostly of oak.

On one of the knolls is the weedy myrtle-
grown graveyard where we have buried our
people for 150 years. Before then, we buried
them where we now forget. We call the knoll
the Graveyard Hill, and the cattle graze
there outside its wire fence and crooked

gate. Higher up on the ridge-top and canting over toward Captain Jim's orchard is a rusty pole set like a crucifix—a television antenna that stands as though it were put there to mark our soldiers' graves. One grave is for Captain Jim, my father's father, who went with the Virginia Rebels; another is for the boy, Elbert Messer, who was fatally wounded in World War I.

Some of the gravestones are too old to read, their names eaten away by time and water; the faint rock-etchings are filled now with gray moss. It is one of these stones that marks the grave of our great, great, great cousin Jacob, who died back in the 1800s when he was just nineteen. Cousin Jacob was sick of the "bloody flux" a long time before he died and used to come up here on the hill to sit under an oak tree and read his Bible. So they buried him under the oak, and for a hundred years it stood there, heavy with age and old funeral keenings, and was called the Jacob Tree. But that tree is gone now, and Little Manfred's tree too, and the willow tree Granny Fanny planted over the grave of her dead baby back in 1875.

But even older than the old graves were the primordial oceans that once covered our fields and cast their seashells into our rock. When the ancient waters receded,

strands of pink and broken coral were left
scattered—as they are still scattered—across
the meadows. This is not coal country. No
rotting swamps lay over these slopes and
upland valleys, only the oceans weaving
and receiving as they laid the pink coral
down: coral rock and white limestone rock,
and the underground streams sucking in
the dark. Through all our generations, we
have picked and hauled corals and piled
them in roseate heaps along the fence rows
and in the swamp.

So it was with us, and is with us still, over
two hundred years and nine generations of
the farm keeping us, and we believing that
we keep the farm. But that is not the way it
is in the real truth of it, for the earth holds
us and not the other way. The whole great
rolling earth holds us, or a rocky old farm
down on Swago Crick.

Until I was sixteen years old, until the
roads came, the farm was about all I knew:
our green meadows and hilly pastures, our
storied old men, the great rolling seasons of
moon and sunlight, our limestone cliffs and
trickling springs. It was about all I knew,
and, except for my father and before him,
the old Rebel Captain, all that any of us had
even known: just the farm and our little village down at the crossroads, and the worn

5

cowpaths winding the slopes; or we kids
driving the cows home in the summer evenings; or the winter whiteness and stillness,
Aunt Malindy's "old woman in the sky"
picking her geese, the "old blue misties"
sweeping out of the north.

Some of our tales were old and old, going
back into time itself, American time. Living
so long there in the same field under the
same gap in the mountain, we had seen,
from our own ragged little edge of history,
the tall shadows passing by. "Old Hickory"
in his coach passed along our dug road one
morning; General Lee one evening on his
way to the Gauley rebel camps. Then, in
1863, as we watched from our cliff walls and
scrub oak bushes, the great Yankee army
passed on its way to the Battle of Droop: all
day long the clank and spur and roll of their
passage, 2,000 3,000, 4,000, hard, blue
Yankees, their bayonet tips made bloody in
the sunset.

Grandpa Tom, our "old one," had gone
with George Rogers Clark to Kaskaskia and
had run the Falls of the Ohio under an
eclipse of the sun. Uncle Bill went to Point
Pleasant against old Cornstalk and his Ohio
Shawnee; then Little Uncle John to the
War of 1812; Captain Jim to the Virginia
Rebels, his brother Al to the Yankees. My
father, in 1906, sailed with Teddy Roose-

velt's Great White Fleet; then Cousin Paul
and Cousin Coe "to make the world safe for
Democracy."

But before I grew up and went out into
the world—and a bloody thing I found it—
we were all at home there in our faded cottage in the meadow, all of us safe and warm.
Sometimes now, a quiet sense comes to me,
the cool mist blowing in my face as though
I am walking through islands of fog and
drifting downhill slowly southward until I
feel the mountains behind my shoulder.
Walking on, I can see the light in the "big
room" window as I come to our cottage
standing in the meadow under "Bridger's"
Mountain, as it always stands on the fore-
edges of my memory, and the old farm where
I ran the April fields and pastures to my
great rock up in the woodland where the
lavender hepaticas grew. Then I knew just
the earth itself: the quiet measure of the
seasons; the stars in the sky; the wheat field
in August, golden: darkness and day; rain
and sunlight; the primal certainty of spring.
Then we were all there together, the years
not yet come on us, these seventy-five years
of war and money and roaring turnpikes
and torrents of blood.

I know, deep down, that our one old
farm is only a ragged symbol, a signet mark
for all the others, the old and far older hard-

scrabble mountain farms of Kentucky, Tennessee, North Carolina, and Virginia, all the briery fields scattered across the mountains south. And how the earth holds us is still a dark question. It is not the sucking deepness that draws us, for the earth is mother, protector, the home; but the oppressor too. It requires, sometimes, the very lifeblood of its own, and imprisons the flyaway dreams and bends the backs of men and women. Yet to love a familiar patch of earth is to know something beyond death, "westward from death," as my father used to speak it.

We could sense, just beyond our brokendown line fences, the great reach of the American continent flowing outward. Because we stood so long in one place, our rocky old farm and the abundant earth of the continent were linked together in the long tides of the past. Because the land kept us, never budging from its rock-hold, we held to our pioneer ways the longest, the strongest; and we saw the passing of time from a place called solid, from our own slow, archean, and peculiar stance.

G.D.'s Sea Chest

It seems the Swago Farm has always been there for me, and fragments of the stories drifting across my mind. How the stories first came to me I cannot answer, for they came in bits and pieces. But I know that I was always there in my small place in the circle and always listening, the scraps and fragments sinking down into my child-mind.

The Indian years were still close to us, and the two Indian graves still lay quiet in our Tommy woodland. The old Seneca Trail, running south from the Iroquois Nation, wound its way across our pastures, and the cows still followed it. It was the same deep-sunken trail that had once been used as an Indian treaty line, one of the long train of broken treaties, so that in those years half of the farm had been white land, the other half red.

So there were Indian stories: the time the big seven-foot Indian came to the Tommy cabin; the day the two Indians came to Aunt

Malindy's and ate her gravy and bread. Or the day the Bridger boys, John and Jim, were killed in the gap of the mountain owned by Mr. Auldridge, so that we always called it Bridger's Mountain, and on summer mornings the turkey buzzards lingered over, floating down-drift on their black, silent wings.

"Save the Farm!" "Save the Farm!" The words ring like a bell up there on Bridger's Mountain, ringing out generation after generation. For more than two hundred years, from 1769 to 1988, our menfolk have farmed the land, walked on it, known it down deep; and each man in his turn has tried to pass the land down religiously, or *more* than religiously, to the oldest son. Each generation in turn must "Save the Farm," then after that it is up to the next man, or sometimes a woman, to take up the task.

First, Grandpa Tom, our first settler, saved the farm—took it, actually—from the Shawnee Indians in 1769, and then went off to the American Revolution to save it from George III. Grandpa Tom took up our land, and Uncle Dock said it was in the springtime, and the chimney stones of Tom's cabin are still scattered over in our Tommy meadow in the thicket of wild plums.

I heard the stories again and again of Captain Jim, my grandfather, the verse-writing, hard-set Rebel soldier, who died right after I was born so we passed each other in the door, and who came back from Yankee prison to save the farm.

Captain Jim lay eighteen months in prison at Fort Delaware. They told how he promised himself if he ever got out alive, he would go home, clear the thorn patch, and build a new house under Bridger's Gap. In prison, he wrote a little brown notebook of love poems and death poems and a long poem called "Virginia Land." In 1865, when the Yankees set Captain Jim free, he walked back to Swago and set to.

Captain Jim built our white house and married Granny Fanny, and when he was fifty-four years old, my father was born. He was named for General George Patton (the grandfather of "Old Blood and Guts," the World War II hero) and for Stephen A. Douglas, and he was called G.D. G.D. was the Captain's only son, his only child, and the old man doted on the boy. As Granny Fanny told it, the Captain taught him to smoke a pipe while he was still a baby sucking on her breast, and pretty soon the old man taught him to chew and spit. He whittled him out a little wooden hayfork and taught the boy to read and write and speak orations, and he planned how G.D. would become a big lawyer and take over the farm.

11

But when G.D. was sixteen, he went off bumming freight trains into the Oklahoma Indian Territory. Styling himself "The Boy Orator of the Allegheny," he had some handbills printed up and traveled over Oklahoma and Texas spouting orations and charging fifty cents a head. Once he orated to six Indians in their lodge house, giving them his best eagle-screaming rendition of "Webster's Reply to Hayne."

For a few years, G.D. would seem to settle down, work on the farm and do some school-teaching, and then he would be off again. As the century turned, G.D. was studying law in Washington City, but he came back to Swago and married Mama. Before my older brother Ward was born, they moved into their own house up at Marlinton, the lumber-railroad boom town that was sprouting on the point of land between the river and Knapps Crick. It was there, in the raw, new lumber town, that G.D. began to practice law.

The great lumber boom was sweeping the Appalachians, and G.D. was elected prosecuting attorney, serving as a *de facto* sheriff, riding the log woods with a pistol in his pocket. But he had started drinking down in Washington City, and when he came to court drunk one day he was disbarred by the other lawyers and then by the state bar.

One evening in 1906, G.D. took the train
to Norfolk, enlisted in the navy, and went off
with Teddy Roosevelt's Great White Fleet.

When G.D. left that January evening
on the "down train" for Norfolk, Mama
held his promises that he would write, send
money, and drink no more whiskey as long
as he lived. But for Mama it was still dead
winter, the house in town was under fore-
closure, she still had little Ward, two years
old, to carry on her hipbone, another child
in her womb sac, and no roof to put over
their heads. She thought of going to Captain's Jim's, but knowing she was not wanted,
turned to her own father's house on Dry
Crick. They could not turn her away. But
she kept thinking of Captain Jim, and in
years after, when she spoke of him, she
would smile.

Her stories, and many others, came to
me of my grandfather, Captain Jim. He had
seen the trumpeter swans passing over, and
in 1830, the wild pigeons with their wings
blotting out the sun. And they told how he
said he had lived to see his only son turned
drunkard and Republican, gone off sailing
with "that buck-toothed Roosevelt's" navy,
leaving the farm and all its hills and meadows to rot and die. The Captain watched
the thorn bush taking the pasture, the fences

13

leaning, the smokehouse falling down. At the last, he had to sell what he called his "woodland-up-the-hollow" to the loggers; and they came in, cut down his oak trees, and left behind them only the bleeding skid roads, the tangles of dying slash.

My mother had heard, through gossips and whisperings, that the bitter old Captain was planning to deed the farm to his nephew, Uncle Dock. So, as soon as my sister Elizabeth was born, Mama took the baby and little Ward and moved in with Captain Jim and Granny Fanny. She was coldly received, but she stayed on. Her name was Grace, and she had come to save the farm.

G.D. sailed around the world for four years. At last, in 1910, after Mama had sold her fleur-de-lis watch to send him train fare home, he came walking and whistling back over the meadows. He had a cannibal's carved eating fork stashed away in his grip sack, the grip he always called his Sea Chest. He kept his Sea Chest beside his chair through nearly fifty years of farming, and bookkeeping, and writing, and teaching, and he could never get the sea out of him.

I never knew the young G.D. who took off for the navy, and I was always told that the man who came back to save the farm

was a very different man. He always seemed
to me as tough as a side of sole leather. He
neither laughed nor cried; he always smoked
his pipe. He hung it in the wry corner of his
mouth and looked out at the world with
cool, dark eyes. He had black hair and dark
skin, high cheekbones and heavy shoulders. When I was a little girl, he would lift
me on his big shoulders and call me Fatty
Jake. I loved the stories he told, stories that
became legends told up and down Swago
Crick of far, far places nobody but G.D.
had ever been.

G.D. told of the day they passed through
the Straits of Magellan, February 1, 1908,
where the Winds of the Williwaw blew
screaming and the glacial fogs swept in. Or
of the morning they sailed into Sidney Harbor in the old U.S.S. *Glacier* and down in
her boiler room the temperature was 140
degrees. G.D. would tell again and again of
the day, off of Tokyo, when a Japanese naval
officer named Tojo came on board the *Glacier* and poked around as though he was
looking for something or had something
in mind.

So the sea was always close to the land on
Swago Crick, and the strange names: Fiji
Islands, Patagonia, Manila Bay. Yet because
the land would never let him go, G.D.
would hitch up old Bird and go out and

15

plow the corn. By the time G.D. had come
back from the navy, my family had been on
the farm so long that it would not let loose
of its people and had its own meanings laid
down in secret under its earth, under the
scattered stones of Old Tom's first cabin,
and under the sweet clover roots of the
Hollow Meadow, under the bluegrass pastures and the corn.

Granny Fanny's
Thorn Broom Handle

*T*he *summer of 1911 was the summer The*
Slashing saved the farm. The Slashing, that
tangled mass of dead braches the loggers
had left on Captain Jim's up-the-hollow
when they skidded away the virgin oak,
had begun to let in sunlight that summer
and had allowed black raspberries to grow.
Even now, seventy-five years later, when I
go home, my sister Elizabeth and I will sometimes speak about The Slashing as though
it were still a living thing. That winter, the
year I was born and the old Captain died,
there was no money and no job for G.D.,
still unable to practice law. G.D. began to
write short stories that winter because he
thought he might get a little money from
them.

He sat late at the kitchen table, writing
sea stories and railroad stories, and two
eerie ones called "The White Dog" and "The
Black Pearl." Then he typed them up on
an old Oliver typewriter he got hold of

and sent them off to the magazines and got them back.

It had been six years since G.D. had touched a drop of whiskey, and he and Mama began talking about him trying for a school job. He would have to take the teachers' examination, and to take it, he would have to go to town. He had no decent shoes and no decent suit of clothes to wear, and so, as he and Mama tried to plan, the new clothes became almost a life and death matter. At last, G.D. talked of selling one of the cows, or of going back to the navy. He kept talking about it, and Mama would cry. But before G.D. could decide, the springtime came, and The Slashing began to leaf out again.

One day when Mama was picking a mess of greens for supper, she saw, spreading across the ruined tangles of the hilltop, some tall white flowers, acres of white flower bushes. When she went to look, she saw that they were black raspberry vines. Mama told that she had never seen such a patch of raspberries, and she would tell it again and again, always, as though The Slashing had been sent by God. The wild birds must have planted the seeds, for usually a slash will come in blackberry vines and fireweed, and the only raspberries on the farm had been a few bushes around the orchard fence.

Black raspberries always sold at a good
price, and as the blooms fell off and the green
berries began to form, Mama watched and
hoped for rain. A good wet season came,
and in July, our miracle: the wild harvest.
The berries ripened juicy and purple-black,
bushels of them; and Mama and G.D. and
Granny Fanny, with my older brother and
sister helping them, went up into The Slashing and picked and picked. I was only a
baby and stayed with Aunt Malindy, and
Mama would come home every few hours
to let me suck. In the evening, they brought
home the great lipping-full buckets and carried them down to Milltown for straight cash.

So G.D. got his shoes and new suit,
walked to town, took the teachers' exam
and passed it. There was a vacancy in the
home school and the trustees decided to
give him a chance. G.D. went to teaching
that fall of 1911 and taught in one school or
another, and later in college, for nearly fifty
years.

When G.D. was seventy-four, his college
gave him an honorary doctor of laws degree, and just for the hell of it, his young
lawyer friend wrote a letter to Charleston
and got the old sailor readmitted to the
West Virginia bar. These legal proceedings
put G.D. into a quizzical frame of mind. A
few laugh wrinkles gathered around his eyes

19

and—as though speaking of the world in general—he made one guarded remark: "It's something of an oddity to me."

In the early years of his teaching, G.D. had some orange handbills printed up and went around the county on another speaking tour. His speech this time was called "The World Through a Porthole," and he would tell the people about geography, and about Cannibal Tom, and the historic passage his fleet had made through the Magellan Straits. He carried his mementos in his Sea Chest and displayed them in faded one-room schoolhouses all up and down the cricks: the boomerang from Australia; the iridescent mother-of-pearl; Cannibal Tom's eating fork; and the great piece of brown and white tapa cloth from out in the Pacific islands of Polynesia and Samoa. The names called softly in the country schoolhouses: Coral Sea, Pago Pago; and on the wall of our best room in the farmhouse, G.D.'s "diploma" hung in its nice frame, bordered with seahorses, and sea serpents, and starry ocean shapes. G.D. got his "diploma" when he had been initiated into the Holy Order of Neptune as the fleet crossed the equator going south. At night by the fire, if I asked politely, I was allowed to look again at the tapa cloth and Cannibal Tom's fork, and I would study intently the postcard picture of Cannibal Tom, riding a bicycle naked. I had

never seen a bicycle, though I had heard
Mama sing about one built for two.

One of my first memories is of Mama in
her Japanese kimono, sitting by the wood-
stove, singing me a song. The isinglass windows on the stove glow red, and on top of
the stove is a shining, silvery decoration
like the steeple on a church. Mama is holding me in the warmth of her kimono—the
only beautiful garment she owns—a Japanese kimono made of palest green stuff,
with white chrysanthemums and pale birds
flying through the flowers. Mama's hair is
loose around her shoulders and falls down
to her waist in a golden-lighted fan. Some-
how, she is not at all the Mama I know day
by day in the kitchen and barnyard, the
work-ridden farm woman in her calico dress,
faded sunbonnet, and ugly Sears Roebuck
shoes. As we sit there, she is singing to me:

> Sweet bunch of daisies brought from
>   the dell,
> Kiss me once darling, daisies won't tell.

Or the song is sad and low:

> Many the hearts that are breaking
> If we could read them all;
> Many the hearts that are breaking
> After the ball.

21

I remember another song Mama would play
on her old "potato bug" mandolin out on
the porch in summer, with our new porch
swing squeaking back and forth. Sometimes
we would get a lemon from town and have
lemonade, and Mama would play:

> Daisy, Daisy, give me your answer true.
> I'm most crazy, all for the love of you.

All day Mama worked over the hot stove
in the kitchen or scrubbed clothes on her
washboard or milked the cows up at the
milk pen. Or she sewed our clothes on her
foot-treadle sewing machine, or in the fall,
rendered out hot lard and canned the sausage cakes. But I always remember the other
Mama, sitting in her pale green kimono or
standing out in the meadow with a wild
pink rose in her hand. For, besides her tame
flowers, her snowballs, bridal wreath, and
thousand-leafed rose bush, Mama knew all
the flowers of the fields and woodlands: the
orange meadow lilies, the purple hepaticas
on the rock, the pale dancing Dutchman's
britches on The Slashing hill, growing there
in the half shade as The Slashing covered
its scars and came to woods again.

There was even a sweet-brier rose, the
English eglantine of the poets, growing on
the wild hillside under Bridger's Gap. It had
escaped from some cabin dooryard; and the

horehound had escaped too, and the sweet
anise, wandering away from the cabins and
running wild on the hills. In later years,
when I too wandered away, I would find
them and cry out their names in recogni-
tion: Sweet William hiding in the grasses of
the prairie, blue lupine I found in the sand
barrens of Carolina, a pink lady slipper in a
Maine forest, tansy by a Massachusetts
cellar hole, or sometimes I can still smell,
blowing east over Hartford, Connecticut,
the scent of cinnamon rose.

The cinnamon rose on the wall of our
farmhouse belonged to Granny Fanny, my
father's mother, and hers too, the row of
bachelor buttons, the pink sweet rockets by
the garden fence. But Granny Fanny had
little time for fussing around with flowers.
She was busy in the kitchen or stable or
running the hills with her gunnysack, picking her loads of wild plums or wormy apples,
or half-rotten kindling wood.

In 1914, the Austrian archduke had been
assassinated at Sarajevo and the world was
engulfed in war, but Granny was not of this
century; she was wild and running free.
Born in 1840, she still roved the rocks and
waste places, tended her ash hopper, which
made lye for her homemade soap, and poured
tallow into her candle molds.

It was as though, standing in her hilly

23

pocket sometime about 1861 or 1862, she had set her thorn broom handle into the world's axis and brought it to a grinding halt. In her long black dress and black bonnet, she walked the hills of another time, and perhaps, even of another country, and gathered pokes of horehound and "life everlasting" to cure the twentieth century of its "bloody flux." She was an old pioneer woman, thin and wrinkled as a dried apple, and with her secret in her that she always kept from everyone. On her back, where she had bent it so long under the burdens, a great knot had grown as big as a wooden maul. In her old age, she wore it like a saddle, the seal and saddle of the mountain woman.

When she was no longer needed in the kitchen, Granny Fanny would go into the fields and woodlands with her gunnysack, or she would take her thorn bush broom and sweep the dirt from the floor of the woodshed, then sweep the path and yard so slick and clean that there was hardly a splinter left. Or she would find a dead sheep out in the pasture, pull the wool off it, pick the burrs from the wool, wash it, card it, spin it, and knit it into crooked mittens and socks. But she would never sew or do fine quilting or mend the clothes. If clothes wore out, she threw them in the fire.

Granny Fanny was not at all a proper

woman like my other grandma, my mother's mother, Grandma Susan, who worked only at housework and wove coverlets and always spoke so nice and fine. Granny Fanny would sometimes have a high fit of temper, pack up her black "gretchel," and go whipping over the hill to Aunt Mat's. She was high tempered, tight-lipped, even, in a sense, an unlovable woman, and yet I loved her with a wild, fierce kind of love and would always fly to her defense. But Granny Fanny had her own sharp tongue, her black "gretchel," and her secret. When I was a child, I could feel that secret in her, and I wanted to know. I wanted to know so much that sometimes, when she tried to sing, I would look at her hard and try to see if her secret was hidden down in the song. Granny was not one for singing and had only one tune. She would sing it in her high cracked monotone, always the song about the little horses:

> Oh, the black and the bay and the
> dapple gray
> And all the pretty little horses.

Sometimes her cracked voice would get to running over and over in my head, and in years after, whenever I thought of Granny Fanny, her song would come back to me like the crackle of thorns in the hearthfire.

Grandma Susan would sing in church: "On Jordan's stormy banks I stand," or "Rock of ages cleft for me"; but Granny Fanny would not go to church, nor to prayer meetings, nor to the pie suppers down at school. The only place she would go was to trade and barter. She would "take her foot in her hand," she said, and whip down over the hill to sell her butter pats or jars of apple butter. She would trade her goods for sugar and coffee and tobacco, for she was still smoking her old corncob pipe, and would carry her store things back home in her sack. If she got cash money, she would put it in her long black leather purse, then stick it under her bed tick to be safe and sound. Granny had never heard of the Protestant Ethic; she was just an uneducated old woman who hadn't learned the evils of working and saving, and she wanted no foolish things— only coffee and tobacco, and her mantel clock with the gargoyles staring out above its face. The only time she ever spent money "foolishly" was the time she went to White Sulphur, a journey of some forty miles, to attend the reunion of Confederate veterans—a trip that was always spoken of in the household as though Granny Fanny had gone to farthest Spain.

White Sulphur was where the Old South had once curtsied on the Greenbrier piazzas, and where the Rebels and Yankees had fought along the road in the desperate August days of 1863. Granny Fanny had helped with the wounded there, and there she first met Grandpa Jim, the old Captain. In 1913, at the reunion, she heard the drums beating again and saw the "Stars and Bars" floating there.

To Granny Fanny, and to all of us in 1913, Captain Jim's war was still "The War." "Back in time of The War," Granny would say; and the Captain's bills of Confederate money were still hidden down in the closet trunk. "Before The War," "In time of The War," we said, as though it had been the only war on earth.

In 1916, we got our first telephone on the farm, and one of the first pieces of news I remember it bringing us was of a new war. It was a big black wall telephone and you could call "Central" with "a short and a long." The telephone man walked by our house every week or so to check the blue glass things up on the poles. The line ran across our farm fields, up Bridger's Mountain, and through the Gap. It followed the old Seneca Indian road, and the telephone wires would sing in the wind. In April 1917, Mama got a telephone call that we had declared war on Germany.

So the Swago boys began to go off to war again: Cousin Coe and Cousin Cliff, Cousin

Paul from up at town; and Elbert Messer and Dennis Cloonan; then Jim Auldridge, from down the river road. G.D. wanted to enlist in the navy, and though Mama begged him not to, he wrote anyway, telling them about his navy years. He felt they could use him, needed him, and when the answer came back that they didn't want him, he was quiet and bit on his pipestem. He was over forty years old.

G.D. went all over the county in the winter of 1917, selling war bonds; and he went up to the train to say good-bye to the boys and wrote to Cousin Coe over in France. Mama knitted khaki hug-me-tights and mittens. We had meatless days and talked about the "Starving Armenians" and "The Huns." One day, when I found a poke of candy out in the elderberry patch, Mama made me throw it away because, she said, the Germans might be dropping pokes of candy down from their airplanes to poison American children.

1918 was the winter of the flu, and when I was better, I knelt down by my bed in my long flannel nightgown to say my prayers: "God keep the boys safe Over There. Don't let the Kaiser kill them. Bring them all home safe."

At night, G.D. would come home with his copy of the *Toledo Blade* and read us the

news from the Marne, Belleau Wood, and
Flanders Fields. And down at the village,
they painted the river bridge from red to
a dull gray color so the Germans could not
see it and bomb it down.

After the armistice, Elbert Messer and
Jim Auldridge came home to die, but Cousin
Coe and Cousin Paul were safe. Down at
school, we learned the poem by heart:

> In Flanders Fields the poppies grow
> Between the crosses row on row
> That mark our place and in the sky
> The larks still bravely singing fly.

Then, almost as suddenly as it had come
to us, the war faded into the past. They
buried Elbert Messer up on our Graveyard
Hill and gave the coffin flag to his mother
for, Mama said, you must never bury the
flag. So Captain Jim and Elbert lay not too
far from one another; and Granny Nancy,
whose father had come over with Lafayette,
lay just inside the rusted gate. Death and
life always run together, so in the last spring
of the war, a little boy was born and named
for the old Captain. We called him Jimmy,
my brother, Young Jim.

With another war behind us and the quiet
years ahead, we were all there at home
under Bridger's Mountain, and Granny
Fanny, eighty years old and her hair sud-

denly bobbed off with "the Flappers," was still running the fields to gather in her pokes of tea herbs: "life everlasting" and penny-royal. When I walked with her across those autumn waste places and heard her speak the name, "life everlasting," my mind kept repeating it. It was a dry, gray ugly flower that lay like a talisman in my heart.

By 1918, most of America had left the old agrarian ways behind; yet down on Swago, down on all the little farms of Appalachia, the mountain geography still closed us inward. Granny Fanny's thorn broom handle was still stuck into the world's axis, holding it tight and strong.

The Door Peg

*B*ecause those years were the years of my childhood, I might tell them in a way that would break my heart. But my heart does not break. There is a kind of benison that falls sometimes on the fields and mountains. Sometimes it is sunlight; or a slow misty rain; or a goose-feather snow drifting down from the sky; and the mountains ringing the fields, ringing the little village down at the crossroads and the white steeple of the Upper Church. And though I realize that I am old now, so that the years play tricks on me, it is all still there sometimes, an unchanged presence, even the rat manure in the water spring; and sometimes we are still at home and it is summer.

There was our old house with its surrounding yards and milkgap and log outbuildings. Then, a mile away, was the little village of Swago with its store and schoolhouse and its four houses all gathered around the crick and Rush Run. The Lower Church

31

was just around the hill, and a mile or so up
the road was the Dry Crick community
with its own white church, called the Upper
Church, and its farmhouses and little hilly
farms. Grandpa Will, my mother's father,
with his neat brown beard and happy blue
eyes, lived up Dry Crick, and he had a seckel
pear tree that he would shake down for us
on summer Sunday afternoons.

Four long miles away was Marlinton,
with its little main street and shaded streets
of white houses, its new railroad track, new
depot, and courthouse square. To the south
of us, about two miles down, was Mill Point,
where the old Cackley Fort had once stood,
where Granny Fanny traded at the country
store and G.D. and I went to grind our
grain at the waterwheel grist mills. Mill
Point was a far journey for us, to be taken
only for trade and flour. Cousin Wint's
store was closer, down at Swago village,
and it was the village and the Dry Crick
settlement that made up the hill-narrowed
neighborhood, the green rocky enclave that
sheltered us and our kin.

We were kin to nearly everybody, married our cousins — like G.D. married Mama —
and clung to each other like a nest of cockle-
burs. All up and down the dirt roads and
footpaths were our kin people: Grandpa
Will and Grandma Susan, Mama's old par-

ents, and all the aunts, uncles, great uncles, great aunts, step aunts, first cousins, second cousins, third cousins, and fourth. We never claimed kin beyond the fourth cousin. Mama's two sisters lived up at town and had running water in their houses and took tub baths.

Every summer at Chautauqua time, when "culture" came to rural America in a tent, I went for a week to visit Aunt Lucy, and Cousin Helen and I could be in Junior Chautauqua, or play hop-scotch, and stroll along the sidewalk eating ice cream cones. And every night we would take tub baths in Aunt Lucy's tub. At home, we had to bathe in a washtub with water out of the rain barrel. There were no comforts such as bathtubs and hop-scotch down at the farm, but the rest of the year I spent there and learned it all by heart.

There were the fields and pastures and Captain Jim's sturdy Dutch cottage. But a dining room and kitchen ell made out of an unpainted sawmill shanty had been stuck onto the back of the house to make more room. Both of the shanty rooms were papered inside with heavy old building paper nailed on with short nails and big round tin caps. The roof of the dining room leaked, and great curves of wallpaper full of rain water

would hang down above the dining table
ready to burst. One of us kids would take
a table fork, climb up on the table, thrust
the fork into the great bubble two or three
times so the rain water would pour out. We
would catch it in the dishpan and hope
that no big rain would come at meal time,
particularly when there was company or
harvest hands. For as long as we lived there,
we coped with this problem in a casual way.
It never occurred to anybody to climb up
on the roof and fix it, for we could always
make do and G.D. was always busy working on writing his short stories, or later, his
civics book. He would sit unperturbed,
writing up an analysis of the Constitution,
as the rain water came pouring down.

We had a fly problem too: no screens,
and long before the time of fly spray. In
summer the flies would swarm black in the
dining room and kitchen and, on a hot and
rainy evening, would cover the ceilings where
they liked to roost. We always had to keep
the food covered or put away in the cup-
board, and we would cover the perennial
dishes of jams and jellies on the dining room
table with an old tablecloth. Just before
mealtime the word would go out to "come
and help me scare the flies," and any two of
us would close all the window blinds in the
dining room, open up one of the outside

doors, and suddenly slam the other. In the darkened room, we would grab up the old tablecloth and a piece of old sheet and beat and flap the air frantically to drive the swarm of black flies before us to the outside door.

The kitchen part of the ell was fairly sturdy and did not leak, though sometimes in summer blades of pale grass might grow through the cracks of the floor. When they did, we pulled them out and wondered at their pale green whiteness, growing there under the dark of the house. Under this open part of the house, we threw our dry midden: dog bones, broken glass jars, bottles, and pieces of broken tools. We threw wet stuff, like leftovers and dish water, into the slop bucket to feed to the hogs.

Around the house was the Little Yard, enclosed with its rough plank fence to protect Mama's flowers from the calves. Outside the Little Yard, in the Big Yard were Grandpa Jim's old log outbuildings: the dug-out springhouse with the log granary up over the top, the chicken house, and out behind the chicken house, the privy with its two square-cut holes. Mama was always mad at Buzz Rogers for cutting the holes square instead of round like in Grandpa Will's privy, which also had pink-sprigged wallpaper and a box of lime.

We milked the cows up at the milkgap

and kept the covered milk crocks in the cold water down in the springhouse. The spring water ran out of a pipe into a wooden water trough that Grandpa Jim had hollowed out with his adz long ago. We churned butter, standing on the stone floor and using an up-and-down wooden churn.

There were two troubles with the springhouse: rat manure from the granary up above kept falling through the cracks of the old logs and down into the water trough where we got our drinking and cooking water, and Grandpa Jim's old drain had been clogged up for forty years.

Every morning, the first one of us to the springhouse would find the bottom of the water trough covered with disintegrating rat turds. Two or three times a day we had to bail all the water out of the trough, wash the turds out, scald the trough with a teakettle of water, then push the trough back in place and wait for the clean water to run. We tried to be careful, but as Granny Fanny said, everybody has to eat a peck of dirt before he dies.

One summer a weasel got into the granary up over the springhouse and the rats ran out and jumped into the limbs of the big apple tree. Hundreds of rats hung there like bunches of black fruit, weighing down the branches of the tree. G.D. and my two

brothers got their guns out and the rats
dropped all around—forty or more of them,
bloody on the ground in front of the springhouse door.

Every time a good rain came, the drain
clogged and the springhouse flooded. All
of us would come tearing, laughing and
screaming and histing up our skirts and
pants legs to wade out into the swirling
waters. We would rescue the crocks and the
tall churn and its dasher and lug them out
under the apple tree until the storm was
over and the water run down. Then we
would sweep the mud and rat turds off the
floor stones and move back in.

The hog pen stood on the hill right above
the springhouse. We took it as a sort of easy
destiny that we would all eat our peck of
dirt. We were never sick either, except with
things like mumps and chickenpox, and
Mama's gallstones. Captain Jim drank the
water for forty-one years and lived to be
eighty-eight; Granny Fanny drank it for
fifty-eight years and lived to be ninety-two;
G.D. drank it, off and on, for fifty-five years
and lived to be eighty-seven; but Mama,
who drank it for only twenty-six years, lived
to be only eighty-two.

The main part of the house that Captain
Jim built was clean and had three of the
rooms wallpapered, one with big red roses

on the wall. After G.D. was able to pay for it, Mama had a big kitchen range, silver-bright with scrollwork and with a big warming oven. Pressed into its door face were the words "Malleable Steel Range Company, South Bend, Indiana."

I learned to read from the newspapers pasted on one side of the kitchen wall and from reading the name on the stove and the name, "Mother" on the oats boxes, and "Arbuckle's Coffee," "Silver Brand Pure Lard," and "Wheeling Steel." Before I was old enough to go to school, my brother Ward and my sister Elizabeth would come home with their books and study by the kitchen table at night under the light of a glass oil lamp. I would climb up beside them, and they taught me to read in Mace's *Beginners' History*, stories about Dan Boone, George Rogers Clark, and "Nolichucky Jack." While Elizabeth and Ward were away at school, I would stand looking out the winter window at the great trees and imagine the hunter men walking there through the shadows until they disappeared through the Cumberland Gap.

G.D. had two cases of books along the wall in the best bedroom: his old school books and stories like *Beside the Bonnie Brier Bush* and *In Days of Bruce*. G.D. always was a soft touch for a book salesman. He said

that an education was the only thing "they"
couldn't take away, and he was always bringing home a new set of books: a green ency-
clopedia, and the red and gold set of Charles
Dickens, and the green and gold set of the
World's Best Literature with hard pieces in
it like ones by Ralph Waldo Emerson and
Immanuel Kant. I didn't like Immanuel
Kant too well, but I liked the Scotch stories,
and especially *Lorna Doone*. I read Dickens,
Homer, Nathaniel Hawthorne, Victor Hugo,
Thomas Hardy, and *The Girl of the Limber-
lost*. Sometimes I would take *Lorna Doone* to
the haymow and read it there, lying in the
soft golden hay of the loft. On rainy days
we played there, jumping and sliding down
the steep slippery hills of hay.

To get into the loft, we put our bare feet
between the cracks of the logs and climbed
up the wall to the door of the mow. The
logs were worn with feet climbing up and,
thrust into the hole of the door, was Captain Jim's old square-knobbed wooden peg,
slick with wear. In a way, this peg was almost a living thing to me. It was just an old
door peg, knotted and familiar and strong,
and it held the door shut. But it fitted tight
into its log as though it was strong enough
to hold together the whole barn, the house,
the fields, the little village, and all our kinfolk spread up and down Swago Crick.

Green-up Time

We had a store calendar on the kitchen wall, and Granny Fanny's old clock on the mantel struck the hours; but time, as we deeply knew it, was hitched to the circle of the year. It was the old peasant calendar, turning with the earth, from winter to spring, to summer, to autumn, back to winter again.

In the late winter season of freezing nights and thawing days, when water began to sing under the ice, and patches of bare ground opened on the south slope, we had "sugar-makin'" in the Woodland-up-the-Hollow. There on the wooded slope stood the sugar orchard, the scattered maple trees that Captain Jim had forbidden to the loggers; and we would set up our sugar camp in the hollow beside the little spring-fed run.

Before the sugar water began to run, we kids, Ward and Elizabeth and I, would get the sugar wood. We would go up on the woodland slope and drag and roll down the windfalls and dead limbs. It was cold and back-tearing work to grab the big end of branches two or three times my size and pull them downhill through the openings of the trees, sweeping behind me snow and dirt and leafy piles. Ward and Elizabeth could wrestle even bigger loads and roll big logs down to hold the fire. It took a lot of wood to boil down sugar water, and there was an old saying: "For a barrel of water, a rick of wood; for a jar of molasses, to boil them good." When dusk came down into the hollow, our work would be done. With our faces and hands scratched, our mittens sodden, and our gum shoes squeaking, we plodded home toward lamplight, hot sup-per, and our homework for school.

When the sugar thaw came, Mama and Granny Fanny would help us drag our sugar-making gear up-the-hollow: bundles of sumac spiles (spouts), two black kettles, the sawhorses, and the sugar buckets. On a flat below the spring were two sturdy forked posts set deep in the ground, and across them lay a heavy sapling set in the crotches of the posts and fastened with baling wire. On this crosspiece we hung our black chains and pot hooks and hoisted up the two big sugar kettles. Up in the woods, Mama trav-eled from sugar tree to sugar tree with the brace and bit. She would pick a new spile-place under each of the biggest limbs to set the bit in, and the pale gold-colored shavings would sprinkle down on the melting snow. The first trickle of sugar water would come from the spile hole and run, darkening, down the trunk. Mama would twist a hollow spile into the hole until it fitted, and hang up the first sap bucket. On days when there was a good run of sap, a tiny stream of water would trickle out of the spiles and the sounds of sweet water would sing in the sunshine and the melting frost runes of the hills.

We kids gathered buckets of sap, moving from tree to tree with our three-gallon buckets. The water sweetened the black pots, and we lit the fire so the sweet water could send up its first wisps of white steam. There was always a big log or two to sit on and rest and watch the fire. We children sat like three ragged blackbirds, dressed in long black stockings, too-small dark coats, and dark stocking caps and black gum shoes. Between bouts of sap collecting, we watched and sniffed the boiling sap water.

Black night would come as the "sweety" began to thicken, and at supper time, we would rake out little beds of coal, five of us, moving busily in our narrow ring of light. We laid thick slices of ham on the sizzling redness and waited and smelled. For dessert, there would be roasted apples, half burned and half raw, and some cane-molasses cookies from a poke.

In some of these years, G.D. was moonlighting as a bookkeeper for the lumber company, and he would come and join us by late suppertime. Then, with the fire in the center and the black hillsides all around us, we waited for the sugar to boil down. When the sweety began to foam up like it would run over, Granny Fanny would take a piece of fat side meat fastened on a stick and run it back and forth to quiet the roiling waves. It was like the wand in my fairy story book: the whiteness would quiet, bubble softly, and begin to "smoke its pipe," breaking the bubbles with brown puffs.

Ward and Elizabeth and I would take our lantern and our tin pie pans and go up on the hill to hunt for a patch of clean snow to make wax balls. When Mama dribbled thickening syrup over the snowy mounds we had gathered, the amber wax would harden into clear, maple taffy.

Mama and Granny Fanny knew all the signs exactly: when to skim off the white, dirty froth; when to run the fatback over the roiling kettle; and when to take off the molasses and sugar. When we were "sugaring off," the hot sugar was stirred and poured into greased pans and "suggins," to be knocked out later, when it was cool, and to be stored high on the pantry shelf for sweetening apple dumplings, oatmeal, and pumpkin pie.

After sugar season, we watched eagerly for signs of open spring. One of the first signs was when Granny Fanny went out to the woods to dig up roots for sassafras tea. She put the red roots and pieces of bark in a pot on the back of the stove and boiled her spicy, red tea. We drank it hot and heavily sweetened, and Granny said it would thin our winter blood.

Soon after sassafras time, it was green-up time, with the first shoots coming up out of the ground. We watched the sprouts hopefully, for this was the time of year for Granny to go to the fields and woods to pick her wild greens, the "sallets" of the old frontier. Granny Fanny taught us all the plants, and how to tell the good greens from the bad. We gathered the new poke sprouts, always being careful not to snip them too close to their poison roots; and we gathered "spotted leaf," leaves of "lamb's tongue," butter-and-eggs, curly dock, new blackberry sprouts, dandelions, and a few violet leaves. Later the white meadow weed would be good, and the shepherd's purse and milkweed sprouts. It took six gallons of leaves to make a mess of greens, and Granny would boil

45

them in the black pot, drain off the pot-
likker, and fry them in hog grease because
there was a saying that poke greens must be
fried in hog grease or the poke would poison
you to death.

Green-up time was also ramp season; but
Mama wouldn't let a ramp come into the
house, for the ramp is a vile-smelling wood's
onion whose odor, like memory, lingers on.
Some of our neighbors and cousins hunted
ramps every spring and carried them home
in gunnysacks to boil and fry. In the spring
down at school, the teacher would sometimes have to throw the windows wide open
to air out the smell of ramps, wet woolen
stockings, and kid sweat.

Sex was never mentioned in our house,
but in the barn and barnyard we learned
early when the cows were in heat—"on a
rippet," we called it—and G.D. would drive
them to some neighbor's bull. G.D. wrote
down on the kitchen calendar when each
cow had gone to the bull, and we turned
the buck sheep in with the ewes. One time
G.D. had a man bring a stallion for old
Bird and told us not to cross the fence or
come near. The stallion nickered and carried on and jumped up on old Bird, but no
colt came. And we saw the frogs breeding
in Grandpa Will's pond, and the rooster

jumping on the hens, and the birds breeding, the butterflies, and even the house flies. Then we hunkered in the barn and sheep shed and watched the bloody borning of the lambs and calves.

The earliest lambs were usually March lambs, and the mothers lay on beds of hay tossed down from the mow. The lambs were wet and wobbly at first but would soon be running out in the stubble field, shaking their long tails and playing chase with one another. Sometimes a bad mother sheep wouldn't let her baby suck, wouldn't "claim it," we said. She would butt him and whirl around from his hungry punching, and he would cry so weak and small. Then we kids would gather him up in our arms and carry him to an old carpet behind the woodbox and feed him bottles of warm milk from the cows. He would become our pet lamb and follow us around all summer, but in the fall we would have to stand by the gate and watch Tom Beard, the cattle and sheep buyer, drive our lamb away with the others to the slaughter pens.

In the spring too, the calves would come and the mother cows had them out in the wild of the pasture, or lying in the shed and looking at us with hurt and feverish brown eyes. The calf would come out slowly, all covered with bloody striffen and clots. Some-

47

times G.D. or Mama or Granny Fanny would have to help the calf out, and one time, when the calf wouldn't come, G.D. cut it up in pieces to save the cow. But usually the calves would stand right up; the mother would lick them off with her tongue, and they would begin to punch around and suck.

One summer I had a pure white calf named Lily, from old Bloss, my pink cow. I taught Lily to lead on a rope all around the yard. In the fall, Tom Beard came and drove her away. But before he did, she had moved deep into my mind, so that there has always been there a calf named Lily, white as the mountain snow.

When we saw our first dandelion, we could take off our long winter underwear. When we saw our first bumblebee, we could go barefoot. Then, Easter would come and we had sugar eggs and beet-pickled eggs and the stormy-colored eggs the rabbits laid. Our cousins up at town found red and blue and green rabbit eggs in their yards. One time, when I wanted red and blue eggs, Ward told me that the rabbits up in town were tame, while our rabbits were wild and laid wild stormy-weather eggs between the bumps of tree roots and in the hollows of rocks up in the pasture. Our rabbit eggs

were either a pale rust color or the color of
walnut-shell dye, with intricate veins on
them like the veins on an onion skin. After
Easter, the spring rains came, and the flowers came to their nooks in the woodland,
and the bluebirds came back to their holes
in the fence posts and gnarly apple trees.
The fence and orchard were alive then with
the flashing, blue, red-breasted birds.

In April the men went out with their
horses and plows to turn the long black furrows. Cousin Rush usually did our plowing
with his big team. The furrow rolled black
and slick-cut from the plowshare, and the
robins would leap down to pull and tug at
the new fishing worms. If we had been lucky
enough to see a bumblebee, we could run
barefoot behind the plow and feel the cool,
soft, spring-smelling earth wiggle between
our toes.

After the fields and garden were plowed,
Cousin Rush would harrow with the old
spike-tooth harrow and, at the last, sometimes haul a heavy wooden drag back and
forth across the fields to break up the clods.
Rush would let me ride on the drag to make
it heavier, and I would slide along, playing
that I was on G.D.'s U.S.S. *Glacier* sailing
into the great Winds of the Williwaw in the
Straits of Magellan.

49

When the oak leaves were as big as a gray
squirrel's ears, it was time to plant the corn.
G.D. ran the furrows with the one-horse
cultivator and let me ride old Bird. I rode
on a sheepskin saddle, with my bare short
legs sticking straight out over the horse's
belly, and I called out in a big Cousin Rush-
like voice, "Whoa," and "Gee," and "Haw."

We all helped with the corn planting.
Each of us had a little bucket of yellow corn
grains to drop and cover up from the crows
flapping up above. We would call out to
mock them:

> Caw, caw said the crow,
> Down to the cornfield we must go.
> Picking up corn has been our trade
> Even since Adam and Eve were made.

We walked along the row measuring with
our eyes and dropped four grains about
every two feet. As we dropped the grains,
we would say the old rhyme Mama had
taught us: "One for the beetle, and one for
the bee; one for the devil, and one for me."

The vegetable garden down the lane was
planted on the same square of ground for
sixty years. The garden had its own essence,
and though the vegetables grew and lived
only in their one summer, certain parts of
the garden remained fixed. These were the
gray planks of the fence and the creaking

lopsided gate, and, in the very center of the garden square, an enormous old tame crab tree with masses of pink and white blossoms in the spring. The crab tree shaded the vegetables, and it was called Captain Jim's tree because he had planted it there long ago. Apple trees grew along one side of the garden, and all around the inside of the fence were scraggly bushes of currants, red raspberries, and gooseberries. In their places were, also, clumps of pieplant, the sage bush, the horseradish plants, and near the gate, one clump of the old-fashioned yellow jonquils we called "Easter lilies."

On garden planting day there was a great bustle of buckets, hoes, rakes, seed packages, robins, fish worms, and sky and earth and sun. If you looked closely at the ground, you could see the tiny red spiders running around, the ones G.D. called "Burpee radish seeds." But we ordered only a few of our seeds from Mr. Burpee. Mama and Granny traded seeds with neighbor women and always kept last year's seeds in a rusty tin box.

All of us worked—hoeing, planting, and lugging in buckets of manure. There were long, rectangular onion beds to raise up above the garden level, and big, flat hills for the cucumbers and the squash. Every seed had its own set kind of hill or row: the potato hills, tall and peaked; the lettuce beds,

narrow and long. There were rows of beans, peas, cabbage, roastin' ears, yellow turnips, and radishes. The garden was always done with the same ritual, for this small square of ground was our main food supply, the source of leather-britches beans, winter cabbage, and potential pumpkin pie.

Later, we would go and watch G.D. plant his tobacco patch. He planted it far off in the wild, on some hillside on the edge of the woods. He burned a brush pile, mulched up the gray wood ashes, and planted the dark microscopic seeds. In fall he cut and cured it, stemmed it, and twisted it to shave off for his pipe bowl or for a hard, twisting chew.

When all danger of frost had passed, we set out the tomato plants Mama had grown in her hot bed. Down underneath the hot bed was the hot horse manure, and on top of the frame were two old cracked window sashes. The hot bed was Mama's special care, and she would grow three or four dozen tomato plants. Until Mama had come to the farm to live, Granny Fanny had never planted tomatoes. She thought they were "pizen" and called them "love apples." But Mama had brought a new way, and even Granny came to eat tomatoes, and Mama would can as many as a hundred quarts for winter use.

We kids went off to the far pasture and
broke off big branches of leafy buckeye
brush to stick at each tomato hill to shade
the young plants. Later, Mama used pieces
of brush to "spray" her tomato patch. When
G.D. got the money, he ordered a brass
sprayer from Sears Roebuck and sprayed
for Mama in the evenings. But the garden
was still full of pests, and we children were
set to picking bugs. We picked red-spotted
potato bugs, and yellow-and-black-striped
and yellow-spotted cucumber bugs, and the
squashy green cabbage worms. I was afraid
of the cabbage worms, for they had two
eyes and, if squashed carelessly, they would
spray their yellow guts right in my face.

May 30th was always Decoration Day.
We call it Memorial Day now and carry
plastic flowers to our grave sites and have
parades and car-wreck killings over the long
weekend. But back then, it was a day only
to show respect to the dead ones of the family, for the dead ones knew and waited for
their flowers. If their living kin should fail
to bring the flowers, then the dead would
know this cold desertion, and the neighbors tell the disgrace.

On the evening before, after the sun had
gone down, we went out into the fields and
woods to gather our armloads of bloom.

53

There were always the white thorn branches
and the dogwood, cross-patterned for Jesus,
and there were pink and orange honey-
suckles (azaleas), wild crab blossoms, and
branches of green laurel. All of these were
carried home and set in buckets of water
down in the springhouse. In the early morning, we would all go to the Graveyard Hill,
carrying our flowers, some old fruit jars,
several buckets of water, and a sickle to mow
off the weeds. As we came to the graveyard
gate, we would feel that strange, empty-
breasted peace that lies over the loved dead.
There were Captain Jim, and Captain Jim's
and Granny's dead baby called "Infant Son
of" and our own little brother who had
never had a name.

We would set our loads down gently—
being careful never to step on a grave—and
would sickle or pull up the worst of the
weeds. We filled the old fruit jars with water
and set a bouquet of flowers at each headstone and each foot, covering the rest of the
grave with flower branches that would shrivel
before noontime, but that, at first, lay fresh
and cool. We laid our branches down quietly,
as though the ones below could almost feel
them and be remembered and remember us
up above.

When our own row was finished, we
would take the rest of the flowers to the old

row of mossy stones where great, great, great Cousin Jacob was lying—the boy who first had been buried here—and we would lay branches on his grave and on the other old graves in the row. Then we would take a branch to each of our newer dead, the aunts and uncles and cousins, and one bunch each to the few neglected strangers who had come, by some chance, to sleep with our kinfolk on the hill.

Soon our living aunts and uncles and cousins would come, gathering in from their cricks and hollows, and by ten o'clock there would be a big reunion in the graveyard, with the men sickling off the weeds, filling in the sunken graves, and talking about crops and weather and what the dead had once said and done. We children would go with our cousins from grave to grave and—being careful never to step on a grave—would read the headstones. Once, when I got to looking absently at Cousin Goldie's forget-me-not hat band, my sister pulled me back and cried, "You've stepped on Little Uncle John!" My foot burned with the sin of it and tears started up in my eyes. But mostly, we would go carefully and earnestly and stand in silence before each headstone, reading the name and dates and whatever else was there: "Beloved wife of," or "He fought the fight, the victory won," or "Asleep

55

in Jesus." On some of the stones were carved pictures of doves and clasped hands and starry shapes. The one I liked best was the lamb carved on top of Cousin Ellis's grave. Cousin Ellis had died of the flu in 1918, and Aunt Nan had had his stone put up with a little lamb lying on the top.

Since before we were big enough to walk, we had been coming to all the funerals. We knew all the crying and the thin, dead faces in the coffins, and the straps being lowered down, and the rattling of rocks and dirt. And we knew, in the wind of the hilltop, the quavering notes of "Abide with me, fast falls the eventide," and "Asleep in Jesus, blessed sleep." We had heard the preacher reading out the words about grass that is cut down and withereth, about the valley and the shadow of death, and the Lord giveth and the Lord taketh away, blessed be the name of the Lord.

As evening came on us from the north-west under the pinnacle rocks, we would gather up our empty water buckets and close the gate behind us. Those evenings, a gray quiet would fall on the Swago Farm for the dead who had once walked the path we walked ourselves back across the mead-ows. Sometimes, as I grew older, it seemed to me that I could feel their empty tracks beneath my own.

Apple Butter Red

After corn planting was over, summer ran hot and fast toward fall. It glimmered in heat waves over the hay stubble and whirred like the jarflies in the tallest trees. The corn-field had to be cultivated twice every season before it could be "laid by," and that was, to me, a hateful task. There were always eight or ten acres of corn rows, thousands of hills, all grown thick with bindweed, ragweed, and smartweed. Every stubborn weed had to be dug out, shaken off, and thrown into the open furrow. But after five rows, we could rest for a few minutes under the apple trees, eating green apples and playing green music on the grass blades we held between our thumbs. As we blew on the grass blades, they whickered in the summer stillness, and the striped chipmunks chattered along the rail fence.

After corn hoeing came haying time, with horses to ride and great frothy buckets of Mama's ginger beer. There was always a big crew of men, our uncles and cousins who traded work with G.D.; and there was the clattering music of the mowing machine, the buggy rake humping its rusty teeth across the field, and the fat shocks hauled in by the plow horses to the stacking poles and the mow.

When the oats and wheat ripened, the cradlers would come with their red cradles and the song of the whetstones began in the early light. Then came the dry song of the swishing grain, the harsh stubble crunching underfoot, and the men racing each other as they cradled the grain into windrows and bound the hot, golden sheaves.

One hot August morning, Snowd Kellison would bring his threshing machine. Its four horses and big red contraptions would come wallowing across our field road, and then the roaring, spewing, and pouring would begin. The men hauled in the wheat sheaves, feeding the great thresher's mouth; the chaff blew out of the chaff-blower, and the wheat grains poured down into the sacks. The men sacked the wheat, hauled it to the granary bin, and poured it into the bin like a golden sea.

At noon, twelve or fifteen men came to the back porch to wash, snorting into the pans of cold water and drying themselves on the roller towels. In the dining room,

the women and girls dished up steaming
bowls of food. The men would take great
helpings on their plates, fork into the meat
dishes with their eating forks, and laugh
and drink buttermilk, wiping their mus-
taches on the backs of their hands. There
would have to be three or four shifts at Captain Jim's long table, the women and children always eating last. On the table would
be three kinds of bread, three kinds of meat,
and big steaming bowls of potatoes, beans,
and corn roastin' ears. For "side dishes," we
had jams, jellies, *schmierkase*, pickles, cole-
slaw, and sliced tomatoes; and, for dessert,
cake and peaches, "floating island," and
blackberry pie with clotted cream.

I always ate in a hurry so I could go out
on the porch and listen to the men talk as
they smoked, chewed, and spit off the porch
edge. Always during these hours, they talked
of the place called Over the Mountain,
where they hunted, fished, and gathered
ginseng. I could see it all rising up before me
as they talked, the hunter men walking
through the trees. Then G.D. would knock
his pipe out, and they would all go back to
the field.

In August too was blackberry picking up
on the pasture hill. We all dressed in men's
overalls, cut off the toes of long stockings,

and drew the stockings over our hands and arms to fend off the cat-claw briers. We would hitch a lard pail around our waists with a discarded belt so we could pick berries with both hands. The briers were fierce; the spider webs clung to our faces in a particularly lecherous fashion, and the towhees fussed and quarreled at us from the thickets for stealing their berry crop. At noon we went to the cow spring to sit on a limestone boulder and eat our lunch of homemade bread-and-butter sandwiches and long strips of cucumber dipped into little paper packages of salt, and we made drinking cups from the silvery green leaves of the tulip tree. By late evening, we could count up that we had made maybe three dollars of our own money for a ticket to the fair and new clothes for school.

Some cold Saturday, we would harvest our winter apples and haul them to the cellar bins. We had "seek-no-farther" apples, "smoke house," "fallow waters," "winesaps," and sometimes a sack of hard, green winter pears. The cellar was full of leaf and apple fragrance, and the leaves rustled as we covered up the bins. Sometimes we would bury a hole or two of apples along with the potatoes, yellow turnips, and cabbages under dirt and leaf mounds along the kitchen yard. We always had the big Apple Butter Stirrin' out at the washplace behind the house. For two days before, all the girls and women of the household, with perhaps a neighbor or two added, would gather on the back porch to peel and core the necessary five bushels of cut apples. The peeled apples were then packed into great crocks in the milkhouse to await Apple Butter Makin' Day.

In the dawn of that hot and spicy-smelling day, the twenty-gallon copper kettle was dragged out of the smokehouse and scrubbed with vinegar and salt. The rinsed copper insides shone pink and gold as we set the kettle up in its iron frame, kindled the fire, and carefully put three copper pennies down on the bottom of the pot. The apple crocks were carried out, and the first batch poured into the kettle with enough water to start the boil. Because apple butter, even with three pennies added, will scorch on the bottom, the stirring, with a long-handled, wooden, hoelike contraption, had to begin immediately. The women and big girls took turns at the hot and arm-aching job.

All day, among the smell of apples and wood smoke, the stirring would go on, as the apple butter thickened and "plopped" and turned a deep, rusty red. Along in the evening, the sugar, cloves, and cinnamon were poured into the boiling pot, and then

61

all the fragrance of the East filled our shabby dooryard, and the children could have a spooned-out sample to taste.

Granny Fanny and Mama would taste and confer seriously, and in the dusk, as the fire died low, one of the men would stroll down to the makin' place and help lift the heavy, hot kettle off the fire. The simmering apple butter was dipped out with a long dipper and poured into the waiting crocks or scalded "air-tight" jars to be stored in the cellar, and darkness would come over the dooryard and the dying fire.

In the late fall came corn-cutting and corn-husking, with fodder shocks and mounds of yellow corn ears lying in the fields. G.D.'s and Uncle Dock's hands would be bleeding and raw from the harsh corn blades, but the golden corn would become hot corn pone and hominy, mush, chicken feed, hog fattener, and always a little left over for the cows. We even used corn grains for checkers, for we could always find a few red ears for our red and gold checker "men."

All fall the men were busy cutting and hauling in the winter's wood, bringing the sheep and cattle in from the hills, doing the fall plow work, and selling the lambs and calves. They hunted squirrel and pheasant up in the woodland, and there would be fried squirrel on the table for breakfast or an occasional grouse or a few quail. In the prosperous years, there would be Mama's prized flock of turkeys to butcher, scald, pick, and pack down in barrels to send off to the Thanksgiving market in exchange for the one big stock of cash money Mama could earn during the year.

At the very end of the fall, often on Thanksgiving Day itself, came the hog butchering, with its shooting, squealing, scalding, and scraping, and with its great piles of steaming hog guts, pink mounds of sausage, grinning hogs' heads, and pans of fresh spareribs and backbone. On butchering day, we children would always retrieve, clean and dry the hog bladders, and blow them up like blood-veined balloons. We called them "footballs" and took them to school to play with. All the kids in school had their own new hog bladder footballs, and we played games of English soccer on the stony, barren school ground.

In winter I sometimes went out early and walked the fields of our farm alone. I liked to go on mornings of fresh snowfall, when all the meadows were trackless and hushed with white. I would walk up through Captain Jim's old orchard and when I got near the moss-gray trees along the rail fence, I would begin to see the little animal tracks and would follow them up and down along the edge of the woods.

There were the triangular prints of the rabbits, or the little field mice tracks like delicate lace woven across the snow. Sometimes there might be fox tracks, one track in front of the other in a straight line. After a warm night, there might be skunk tracks, like little human footprints but with a soft white dab where the tail had brushed the snow; and up in the bushes the bird tracks made dark little stitches mending the hill. There were also the round cat tracks, no claws showing, the soft, retracted feline tread; and one morning I saw blood on the snow.

Sometimes I could feel the others close around me, down in their little burrows in the earth: the gray, sleeping wood mice; the little striped ground squirrels; and the soft curled-up rabbits, the snoring old groundhogs, and the ring-tailed raccoons. Then the silence would come down, as though it fell on our meadows from the high whiteness of Pinnacle Rock.

Neighborhood Ways

The Swago neighborhood was interlaced with wagon roads and with little footpaths that wound and sprangled across the hills. The Big Road that ran through the village, following the old Indian Trail, was not hard-surfaced until the late twenties. There were also smaller dirt roads: one down the river, one up Dry Crick, and the one across the river bridge. We were, essentially, a foot-walking society; and the paths intersected farm fields, ran up over pasture hills, along fence rows and the winding cricks. All paths and roads led eventually to the village, and there were the three centers of our life: Wint's store, the two-room schoolhouse, and the Lower Church just around the hill. The Upper Church stood at a crossroads up on Dry Crick.

The store, which was also the post office, was where we got our mail, did our trading, picked up the news of the week, and visited

with our neighbors and kin. There, the
men sat around the stove, or on the store
"platform," talking, chewing, and spitting.
On clean-up day, Wint would have to take
a shovel to the dried tobacco spit, sort of
scaling it off like he was digging up a hard-
packed garden in the spring.

The store building was a long cavernous
structure, with only a little light filtering in
from the high windows in the front and
rear. In this narrow darkness, Wint kept a
wild assortment of store goods in stock.
There were showcases full of neckties, arm-
bands, rolls of ribbon, button cards, rifle
bullets, and shotgun shells. Horse harness,
oil lanterns, steel traps, and gum boots hung
from nails along the wall; and there were
pepper boxes, vanilla bottles, cheese, fireworks, Arm and Hammer soda, yard goods,
wooden buckets of salt fish, women's "fasci-
nators," Fig Newtons, and high-buttoned
shoes. Wint also took in products from the
neighborhood as trade goods: eggs, prints
of butter, pokes of ginseng, maple sugar
cakes, berries in season, and in the winter,
the stretched and aired skins of foxes, raccoons, possums, and skunks.

Various odors mingled in the smoky air,
but the two that gave the pungent essence
of the store were the brown Brazilian fragrance of coffee, and the stewing brown

smell of tobacco juice. To a mountain child,
these odors gave promise of a five-cent tab-
let for school, a poke of striped peppermint
candy, or even a box of Uneeda Biscuits or
a can of sardines. We particularly envied
our cousins, Wint's four children, who could
come freely into the store, open a can of tomatoes, pepper it, and drink it down for a
quick lunch. The tomatoes Mama canned
at home lacked the exotic flavor of the store
brand. In all cases our homegrown and
homemade products seemed inferior to us,
and we would refer favorably to "store
cheese," "store cookies," "store peaches,"
and "store clothes."

Over this wild profusion, Wint presided
as entrepreneur. He was a natural store-
keeper, canny, warm, persuasive, and gifted
with a poetic and prodigious wit. He would
stride up and down the store platform, bead-
ing down on the floor nail heads with shots
of tobacco juice and summing up the eccen-
tricities and equivocations of the neighborhood in highly colored phrases. In a sense,
Wint held the neighborhood together, like
my peg in the haymow door. For Wint had
charisma, a kind of red-headed Irish power
to attract, to hold, and to finish off. If a
world problem arrived in the weekly copy
of the *Toledo Blade*, a war or a diplomatic
crisis, Wint could finish it off with the same

quick dispatch he used on a mangy hound dog sniffing around his salt fish kegs. The store was kept open from early morning to late at night, and it was for all of us, but most of all for the men. They would sit, and as their spit fried on the stove, world problems, and old guilts and ancient sorrows would fade away.

The schoolhouse stood about a hundred yards above the store on a patch of dry, rocky, crick gravel we called the playground. The Big Road ran on one side; Rush Run along the other, and up on the laurel-banked hillside canted the two wooden privies. Two well-worn paths led uphill to these sanitary and social centers, and under a hemlock tree by the run was the girls' playhouse of flat rocks.

The schoolhouse, one of the best in the county, was painted white and had an imposing bell tower and two classrooms, one called the Little Room and the other the Big Room, with two rooms for storing dinner buckets and two long cloakrooms with rows of metal hooks. Each of the two schoolrooms had a big pot-bellied stove, rows of fastened-down desks with ink wells, two well-worn blackboards, and a shelf of books. Up front was the teacher's desk and, facing the teacher, the Recitation Bench where we lined up to recite. On two sides of the room were several windows with ragged, incorrigible window blinds. There were erasers and chalk, a metal waste basket, a picture of *The Landing of the Pilgrims*, and out in the hall, a metal water cooler. Outside stood the flagpole, and every morning some favored student would be selected to run the flag up.

When the bell rang from the tower, the teachers would stand at the top of the steps in front of us, and the Big Room teacher, the principal, would call "attention" as we lined up, clapped our legs together, squared our shoulders, saluted the flag, and then marched up the steps and into our rooms. When the teacher came in and stood behind her desk, we would stand and sing "My Country 'Tis of Thee" for "opening exercises." On the last verse, the teacher would hold up a warning finger, and we would all sing very softly. After a story or Bible reading, the teacher would call the roll. Some of our teachers had us answer our name call with a Bible verse: "I will lift up mine eyes unto the hills, from whence cometh my help"; or "The words of a man's mouth are as deep as waters"; or the favorite short one, "Jesus wept."

In the Little Room, we had twenty or twenty-five pupils and there would be about ten or fifteen minutes for each class: reading, arithmetic, spelling, English, and penmanship. Each class in turn would file up and sit on the Recitation Bench. For spelling, we lined up against the wall, had a "head" and a "foot" of the class, and "turned each other down." Sometimes, we read history stories like "The Pilgrim Fathers," or "George Washington and the Cherry Tree," or the story of George Rogers Clark's men drinking deer broth on their way through the swamps to Kaskaskia. When I was six and in the second grade, we learned the names in alphabetical order of all our state's fifty-five counties, and of all the forty-eight states.

When we got up into the Big Room, we had regular classes in geography and history, and in "physiology and hygiene," "agriculture," and "civil government." Our history stories were about "Nolichucky Jack," Christopher Gist, Francis Marion the "Swamp Fox," and Concord Bridge. In our big readers were many of the Greek myths. We read "Pandora's Box," the story of how evil and hope came into the world; the story of Proserpine and Pluto, of Theseus and the Black Sail, and of Jason and the Golden Fleece.

Sometimes on Friday afternoon we would have "recitations" from the floor. We said poems like "The Midnight Ride of Paul Revere," or "Old Ironsides," or "Westward, westward Hiawatha / Sailed into the fiery sunset / Sailed into the purple vapors / Sailed into the dusk of evening. . . ."

On winter mornings after we had waded a mile or two through the snow, we would sit on the benches around the stove to dry our feet and clothes. The room was cold, and steam would come up from our sodden shoes and stockings; the smells of wet woolens and long underwear, of onions and floor oil mingled in the room. At noon hour we would hurry up with our cold sausage sandwiches and rush out on the school ground to play in the snow. We would have snowball fights, slide on the crick ice, play Fox and Geese in a snowy ring, and coast on our wooden sleds down the river road. About 1917, when lumber-mill prosperity hit the village, my brother Ward had a second-hand sled with the words Flying Arrow painted on it in red and blue. When the coasting was good, we might come back at night, build a fire down by the bridge, and coast until ten o'clock. Then we would walk home, pulling our precious sled behind us up Uncle Dan'l's hill.

In good weather, when noon hour and recess came, the big boys played paddleball with a yarn ball, or football with their blown-up hog bladders, or sometimes they would play Run, Sheep, Run. The girls and little boys played Drop the Handkerchief, Pet Squirrel, Skip to My Lou, or Green Gravel, Green Gravel.

Sometimes the teachers had trouble with kids who went into the dinner bucket room and stole food out of the pails. Or boys would dip the girls' long hair down in the ink wells or draw dirty pictures or pass dirty notes. If kids got into fights, they might get a whippin' or have to stay in after school. Sometimes, they were shut up in the cloak-room for half a day or ordered to write some moral motto a thousand times, like "For Satan finds some mischief still for idle hands to do."

Sometimes some kid would get infested with what we called the "seven year itch," or a girl would come to school with "nits" in her long hair. Then the whole neighbor-hood had to rub with sulfur and grease or comb their hair out with doses of lamp oil. In the fall we often got "diphtheria sores" that would bleed and run, and we would have to take a dose of Epsom Salts every morning before breakfast for seven days.

The most important thing to us girls was that the teacher should be pretty and wear nice clothes. We would think about it all summer, wondering if the teacher would have a pretty dress. One year in the Big

Room, we had Miss Anne Correll. She was
nice-dressed and "modern," and she had
the board of education put in a new, flat-
topped stove. Then she told us to bring
cabbage, potatoes, and onions from home,
and she put them in the pot and made us
"hot lunch." For Valentine's Day, Miss Anne
pasted red hearts and let us have a Valentine Box. Sometimes, she would use colored
chalk on the board, and for Christmas
she drew a border of red and green holly
and red bells around the top of the black-
board and pasted Christmas trees on the
window. Miss Anne had a subscription to
The Normal Instructor and Primary Plans and
she took pictures out of it and programs for
Christmas.

We always had a night Christmas program at the schoolhouse. We would have a
tree decorated with strings of popcorn and
teaberries and red paper chains. The presents
were put under the tree, and the bracket
lamps lighted, and the stove boomed up
until it glowed red. We all wore our best
clothes, and we girls had our hair curled in
ringlets (on rag curlers) and we had ribbons
in it. The kids in the program would hide
in their costumes out in the cloakroom until
the crowd gathered on the small, crowded
seats. Little girls dressed in long cheesecloth
robes carried candles and sang "Away in a

73

Manger," and we said poems. At the last would come the pageant, with the baby Jesus lying like a china doll in his straw crib; and little shepherds dressed in sheepskins and little wise men in their sisters' long dresses with tinsel on their turbans; and then little cheesecloth angels with gold cardboard wings.

When the last little shepherd had gone from the stage, Tone Lightner, our village blacksmith, would come in his big Santy Claus suit and give out the presents. Tone was jolly and good, and he always came in acting like he was all out of breath because his reindeer had given him a little trouble. Once when he fell on the footlog crossing a stream, he came in all bloody, with his suit and whiskers torn, and he told us his reindeer had run off with him and nearly spilled the sleigh.

At the schoolhouse too we had neighborhood cake walks, pie suppers, and box suppers. The box was usually a decorated shoebox full of fried chicken, cake, and pickles. The pies were in boxes too, all covered with crepe paper and cut-out pictures or tinsel bows. The big girls worked and agonized over their boxes, for the boys would bid on them when Tone Lightner auctioned them off. The boys who got the boxes would get to eat with the girl whose name was hidden

in each box, and the money went for a new
dictionary for the schoolhouse, and later,
for a playground swing.

On Swago Crick, both of our churches
were Methodist, one a Methodist Episcopal
and the other a Methodist Protestant. There
was no noticeable variation in faith or ser-
vice, and the people of the community at-
tended both. The churches were both white
frame buildings, and both had dark var-
nished benches, a raised platform and altar
railing, oil lamps in hanging brass brackets,
long wood stoves, and wheezy foot-pump
organs. Neither had a full-time preacher,
but both were served, off and on, by a cir-
cuit preacher who came every second Sunday, or as rarely as once a month. Other Sun-
days we had Sunday school, sometimes in
the Upper Church on Sunday morning and
in the Lower Church on Sunday afternoon.

The Upper Church was distinguished by
its high bell tower and, much later, by its
two privies out behind. Porter Kellison was
the Sunday school superintendent and led
the singing, and Aunt Edna or Nellie Kellison played the organ while Dorsey Little
passed the plate.

We kids would get dressed on Sunday
mornings and Mama would give us each a
penny to take to the Korean orphans. She

would tell Elizabeth and me to tie our pennies in the corners of our handkerchiefs so as not to lose our offerings; then we put on our decorated straw hats and walked barefoot down the lane on our two-mile road to Sunday school. We always carried our shoes and stockings to "save them." When we got to the culvert just below the church, we would sit down and carefully put on our stockings and our white canvas Sears Roebuck slippers that had been cleaned on Saturday with Old Dutch Cleanser and set out in the sun to dry.

The church bell rang out over the valley, and when all the people had come in and sat in their places, Nellie Kellison went to the organ and Porter Kellison got up to lead our first hymn. It was often "Oh, Come to the Church in the Wildwood." We would all "rare" back and sing at the top of our lungs, for we put more stock in volume than in modulation for praising God. When we came to the chorus, Porter Kellison and Grandpa Will would come in strong on the bass: "Oh come, come, come, come," and the great deep "comes" would roll out the open door as though calling all the world home.

My Grandpa Will could read the old shaped notes in the hymnbook for, way back, he and Mama and Grandma Susan had all gone to Singing School. Grandpa

Will said family prayers, and said grace at
the table three times a day. He gave money
to the church, helped keep the building re-
paired, and read his Bible. He believed that
when we all died, we would meet again in
Heaven: he and his father and mother,
his six brothers and two sisters, all their
children and grandchildren, and all the
kin and neighbor folk, gathered together
where Jesus had gone to prepare a place
with golden stairs and no sin nor sorrow
nor parting. Grandpa Will would lift up his
head, and his blue eyes would look far away
as he sang: "Yes, we'll gather at the river,
the beautiful, the beautiful river / Gather
with the Saints at the river that flows by
the throne of God."

The summer I was eleven, we held a daily
Vacation Bible School for the little children at the Lower Church. It was a new
thing and a lady came in from way-off to
hold the school. Hiram Barns, who lived in
a neat painted cottage just above the village
and was active in church, had helped with
all the plans. The lady's name was Miss Virginia, and Mr. and Mrs. Barns had her to
stay with them and fixed their spare room
all nice for her. Since I was a big girl then,
I helped Miss Virginia with her teaching.
She had colored paper and crayons for the
little kids, and new songs to teach, and a

little play to put on. I went down to the
church every morning, and I loved Miss
Virginia. She had a nice soft voice and curly
hair and wore lace on her white blouse. I
read to the little kids and helped them with
their songs. Miss Virginia let me take them
outdoors, where we sat in a circle on the
grass near the graveyard, and I read them
stories about Jesus. The children got to take
their pictures home, and on the last day Miss
Virginia had a program so all the mothers
could come to see.

When Miss Virginia told us good-bye, I
almost cried and could think of no one else
for a week. Later, we began to hear things
about her. It turned out that Miss Virginia
had gone away and written a bad story about
us in a church magazine. Hiram Barns was
a subscriber to the magazine; and when it
came, there was a story about the community of S———, by Miss Virginia. In the story
she told how it was up in the mountains,
how ignorant and crude the people were.
She told about Hiram Barns's house and
made fun of it and of how Mrs. Barns dipped
snuff. Hiram Barns passed the magazine all
around the neighborhood, and we all read
what Miss Virginia thought about us. I felt
sorrow and disillusionment, and, for the
first time, I began to wonder about the people
beyond Swago Crick.

For all the years of my childhood, our little neighborhood centered on the store, the schoolhouse, and the church, and the narrow roads and paths that ran up and down. Once every summer, we went down to the little railroad flag stop and took the one coach train to town to visit our relatives there. Still our village pattern held, and we walked down over the hill to the store or up Dry Crick to the church night-meetings. Coming home with our lantern through Uncle Dan'l's woodland, we could sometimes hear the small animals scrambling off in the woods or see a piece of foxfire shining at us from an old, rotten log. When we went through the gate at the barn, I always felt the peg set solid in the haymow door, and then old Jack or Shep would begin to bark, and I could see the panes of lamplight shining through the night.

Signs and Portents

*A*unt Malindy *was no kin of ours, but all* through my childhood she stayed at our house, a free boarder who always sat in our best rocker. She was very old and very fat and always wore her shining fat dress of black sateen; and she ate enormously, never did a lick of work, never even peeled an apple or snapped a bean, and I loved her and lay safe and warm, pillowed against her sateen breasts.

G.D. always said that she was there because she had no other place to go to; but we never thought why she was so welcome, so well come. We didn't even think to wonder, for she was our Seeress, the Priestess of the Swago. She made the prophecies, the telling of daisies and the writhing of mystic serpents; and she had all the children to rock.

Aunt Malindy was full of signs and portents. She had her death-bell sign, her howling hound dog, and, from her girlhood, that strange, death-ridden omen which she

had seen one long-ago summer midnight:
the great fireball screaming in the sky over
Buckley Mountain the night her brother
Potts was killed at the Battle of Gettysburg.

It's a strange thing about old tales and
superstitions: you believe them and you
don't. You know that deep down in the
depths of them they are as true as the morning, but that all the glittering, eerie surface
is as false as false. Nobody comes to visit because you drop a dirty dishrag, but you keep
your dishrag clean. And no snake stings a
tree to kill the tree, but back in the Garden,
his eyes were as green as glass.

There were so many snake stories that
they crawled slowly on the edges of a child's
sleep. To begin with, Satan had gone into
the Garden in a snakeskin, and now the
black snakes sucked the eggs in our chicken
house, and it was rumored that they sometimes sucked the cows. The snake stories
were most often Aunt Malindy's; but they
could be Uncle Dock's or Cousin Rush's or
the true one G.D. told. Aunt Malindy told
how her sister Mag had been charmed by a
beautiful red and blue circled viper whose
eyes fixed on her so she couldn't move. At
last a dog ran between her and the snake
and broke the spell. Aunt Malindy's other
sister had been bit by a copperhead in dog
days, and every year after that, for fifty

years, in dog days her sister's leg would swell up and mottle with red, coppery spots.

Mad black snakes smelled like cucumbers. Hoop snakes with horns in their tails would put the horns in their mouths, roll down the hill, stick their tail-horn into a tree trunk and the tree would die. And there were glass snakes. When you hit them, they flew into a million pieces and then went back together again. One summer Sunday morning, G.D. had come upon a whole nest of copperheads by a shale cliff on the riverbank—a tight, writhing coil, and others crawling around lifting their arrowheads. He cut a strong willow withe and slashed and slashed until he sickened from the venomous smell. Then he walked back up the road to church and brought some of the men to see. When they stretched the dead snakes out on a flat rock, they counted a hundred and twenty-three.

There were panther stories too, and always, just over the Pinnacle, lay the dark mystique of the wilderness with its feral footpads and yellow-green eyes. There was the panther that had followed Mama's buggy through the pine forest over at Pickens, and the panther that had gone to sleep in the cattle scales. They told that Cousin Joe Buckley kept a pet panther who slept with him every night tame as a cat, until one night when Joe awoke to teeth pinching his throat.

Sometimes, at our sugar-makin' camp-fire, G.D. would tell of the night Grandpa Jonathan-the-Elder fell asleep by his sugar fire and a panther came up and sniffed his face. Grandpa Jonathan lay very still and played dead; and the panther scratched around, covered him up with leaves, and left him cooling there. Grandpa Jonathan jumped up, filled a kettle with firebrands, and started to the Tommy cabin; but he heard the panther following him and could see his eyes in the night. Everytime the panther moved close, Grandpa Jonathan would throw a burning brand, until at last he got safe to the cabin. Next morning when he got up, a little skiff of snow had fallen; and there, on the outside of the window sill, were the prints of the panther's forepaws where he had reared up to look in at Grandpa through the pane. In the dark night, after we had sugared off and were trekking wearily home, I often wished for a little kettle of burning firebrands. Behind me, in the dark, I could always sense the sneaking, yellow shape and feel its green slanty eyes.

We had taboos, and a lot of them had good reason: Never stand under a locust

tree during a lightning storm. Never eat a
bite of food in the privy house, for every
bite you eat there you feed to the Devil. Do
not pick up toads for they give you warts.
Do not play in the fire or with matches, or
you'll wet the bed that night. Never touch a
thousand-legged worm. Never kill a lady-
bug or your house will burn. Never kill a
news bee or you'll get bad news. Never milk
on the left side of a cow. Never bellow at a
mad bull. Don't sleep in the light of the full
moon, or you'll go moon-mad and turn blue.

If a cow is bewitched and won't give her
milk down, sprinkle salt and pepper on the
root of her tail. If a dog howls at night, a
soul is passing. When the "death bell" rings
in your ears, no one else can hear it. When
you hear it, you will die. Always cut your
brush in the dark of the moon. If you can't
find your cows, talk to a grandaddy spider
and he will point one of his front legs to
show you which way they've gone. Yellow-
root tea will cure a sore throat; a piece of fat
side-meat tied on your foot will draw out a
thorn; stump water is good for flea bites
and running sores.

Aunt Malindy and Mama both had their
old songs and ballads; and, in summer when
the men were away, we would sit on the
porch in the evening and sing together, or
we would sing snatches as we worked:

> Where have you been, Lord Randall
>   my son?
> Where have you been, my own dearest
>   one?

Or:

> A carrion crow sat on an oak
> Fol do riddle de, Lol de riddle de
> High ding doe . . .

Or Granny Fanny's thin monotone would quaver from the shadows: "Oh the black and the bay and the dapple gray."

From Aunt Malindy, and from Uncle Dock too, we had the lore of the fields and woodlands, as we ran their paths in summer and made up our games. Never look in a bird's nest or the baby birds will die. Weasels kill to suck the blood. A red squirrel will eat off the private parts of a gray squirrel. Talk to a doodle bug down in his dung hole, and he will tell you the secret of the earth.

We saw the baby skunks walking along in a straight row behind their mother, perfectly disciplined and with their little tails waving back and forth in rhyme. And we watched the chipmunks frisking along the fence rows, found the soft baby rabbits in their nests. Never touch a baby rabbit. Never kill a buzzard. If you see an owl in the daytime, bad luck will come before dark.

Once, G.D. took me out to the smokehouse to see the big white owl. I must have
been three or four and he came and woke
me up. He picked me up, wrapped me in a
blanket, and carried me outdoors. Something had been killing our hens that roosted
on the "plate" of the log smokehouse, and
G.D. had set a trap. It was a cold, snow-
covered night, and I remember the snow
and the great white owl there in the lantern
light. His eyes were big and golden and had
fiery streaks in them. I looked at him, and
he looked back at me. I felt his hate and his
fear. He seemed to be looking at me alone
and asking me a question I could never
forget.

Up at the cow spring, we whittled out
water wheels, set them in the rushing water,
and watched them whirl around. We whittled
out wooden boats too, and set them adrift
on the flood: "Boats of mine a-boating /
When will all come hone?" Or we made
beautiful cornstalk canoes, or clay pipes
from the blue rock we found cropping out
along the ledge. In spring we would make
willow whistles from the willow withes. We
slipped the bark and cut holes in the sides
so they could whistle their April tunes.

We played Buckeyes with the nuts of the
buckeye tree, a scrubby type of horse chest-

87

nut. Because of their coloring and general fat slickness, buckeyes made perfect white-faced cattle. We removed them from their husks, polished them to a shining glow, and gathered them into "herds" on the great limestone rocks. Sometimes I played at driving my buckeye cattle in a great lowing herd to the Indian battle down at Point Pleasant; or, like Captain Jim, to market over at Staunton, Virginia, across Bull Pasture Mountain. My fat herd would wind along the leafy forest roads, and I would be behind them on my high-headed black stallion, winding through the autumn shadows until we disappeared forever into the trees.

We skipped rocks, hurled apples from long green withes, rolled rocks down the hillside—careful not to kill a cow—or twisted groundhogs out of their holes with a forked stick. We played a more dangerous game with Auldridge's old roany bull. He was on one side of a leaning rusty wire fence; we, on the other. We would put our fists through the wire and push him in the head to make him mad. We were so close I could smell his breath and see the curly hair on his forehead, the little black flies crawling in the corners of his rheumy eyes. We dared each other to taunt him until he got mad, backed up, and began to paw the ground. We took off then, but I can still see his red eye-corners with the black flies crawling in them, like the He-Beast, the Minotaur out of my grade school reader, who lived in the Cretan Labyrinth and ate the seven youths and seven maidens every year.

Often as we grew older, Ward and his best friend Jess would go off fishing or setting "cat" hooks, and Elizabeth and I would play "playhouse" up on the rock cliffs. We gathered armfuls of green moss and spread it for rugs on our floors. We made little chairs and sofas of rocks and spread these. Then we would serve tea in acorn cups and saucers, talk "lady talk," and wear decorated hats. Elizabeth was the town "milliner," and we would gather a big weed leaf that grew nearby, called hatweed, about as big as a rhubarb leaf and about that droopy shape. Elizabeth would fasten the hat leaves together in the back with a sharp thorn and decorate them with hillside flowers, the ones her "customers" used for money: oxeye daisies, black-eyed Susans, wild roses, and pink milkweed bloom.

In late summer, when the long, delicate green milkweed pods were full, we would strip off the outer pods and carefully take out the silky white insides. These were our "milkweed ladies," as pure and delicate as soft white dove-birds, there on our rock cliff in the sun. We would invite them to

"tea," a crowded three of them sitting so
ladylike on our moss sofa; and we, in our
millinery hats, serving them. We would tell
them in high-pitched Southern voices, about
the Ladies' Aid meetings and the straw-
berry festival down at the church; and one
day I made up a rhyme:

> Milkweed ladies so fair and fine,
> Won't you have a sip of my columbine?
> Or a thimble of thimbleberry wine?

As we talked and laughed, the golden finches
that frequented the thickets flashed back
and forth, and their gold and black wings
caught the slants of sun.

Sometimes Mama came up to our "house"
and visited us, and we would show her our
flower hats. When Mama was a girl, she
had dreamed of being a milliner, sitting in a
fine shop somewhere and sewing flowers on
beautiful ruffled hats. Sometimes now, I can
still see her standing there on the hillside
with a wild pink rose in her hand. To her,
through all life's tragedies and brute labor,
the flowers waited with their sweet surcease.
On Sunday afternoons, she would go with
us to the woodland or over into the meadows and find the wild flowers, in their season, full in bloom. In earliest spring, we
found the arbutus hiding under the leaves
and last snowfall. Then the white blood-

root opened, and we found Jack-in-the-Pulpit on the edge of the wood. In June we went to the Indian graves to find the pink moccasin flowers; and in autumn we found the bluebottle gentians by the swamp. On the mossy cliff up in the Little Woodland were the lavender and blue hepaticas that bloomed in April; and all around them, on the moss of the rock, the trailing long-hearted leaves of the walking fern, the frail ebony stems of maidenhair.

Sometimes, I went with Granny Fanny to gather her medicine tea in the run-out field over near old Tommy's cabin where the sedge grass and the briers and thistles grew harshly from their worn-out earth. But growing there, all winter, were the dry austere blooms of the pearly everlasting, the "life everlasting" that Granny took home to boil for a fragrant, half-bitter tea. From Aunt Malindy, what I kept was her fireball screaming above the Buckley Mountain the night her brother Potts was killed. But it was the *name* of Granny Fanny's flower that I loved and remembered and kept with me; the "life everlasting," living there above the winter, beyond the storms.

Over Bonnie

*O*nce, *fifteen million acres of virgin forest*
stretched from the top of the Allegheny
range to the Ohio River shore; and, when
I was a child, G.D.'s and Uncle Dock's part
of it ran for sixty unbroken miles beyond
our Pinnacle Mountain: a quarter million
acres of hardwood forest. For over a hundred years, our menfolks and all the other
Swago hunters walked it as though it belonged to them.

Every spring and every fall, G.D., Uncle
Dock, Cousin Rush, and my brother Ward
took off Over the Mountain for their fishing trip to Cranberry River, to Williams,
and Gauley, and Black Mountain Run. It
was a fifteen-mile trip into the wilderness,
and the day before Mama would make up
eight or ten bread flat cakes, while we children dug several hundred slithery fishing
worms and packed them into Prince Albert
tobacco tins. Among the doubtful prophecies of weather, G.D. and Ward would pack

up their old haversacks, Mama's big tin frying pan, the red snuff boxes for farmer matches, the blackened tin bucket for boiling coffee, and two or three big cloth sugar sacks to carry the fish home in. At the very last, they strapped the fish rods on, and the pocketknives, hooks, and leaders. They took no map, and no compass. Though they were forever getting lost in some alder thicket, they must find their direction by the lay of the land, the flow of the waters, the shadows, or the star.

It would be just before dawn as Mama, Elizabeth, Granny Fanny, and I draped on the yard fence to watch their four misty shadows humping one after another up our pasture slope. They disappeared northwest into the forest. I knew I could never go with them, but I followed them still in my mind. Down in my heart, I knew every trail and wood sign from learning them by the fireplace in winter, and on the porch at harvest noon. I knew I could walk it blindfolded: the steep open trail up to Beech Spring; then into the forest again; north past the overhang of High Rocks; down onto the wild headwaters with the forest around me, darkness at midday, the great oaks and the deep pavilions of shade. If the men went by way of the Gallegly, I could look down and see the rolling savannahs of bluegrass, mile

upon rolling mile of open grassland sweeping down to the forest and river shore. As I had learned it, I had learned it deep: the farthest place, the ultimate passage.

All morning long, as I helped Mama with the milking and the hogs and chickens, I followed the men northwest. I could see them clearly, sitting by their campfires in the evening, their beds of moss spread out for the night, the brook trout frying in the pan. I knew they would be telling how they heard the wind and the sounding water; and the stories again about Captain Jim's time, or even back to Old Tom's time when panther had roamed Over the Mountain, and Old Tom had seen the eastern bison in small droves, great shaggy black-humped bison coming down at sunset to cross the ford.

Over at home, the week was a long and dreary one: the garden to tend, the cows to milk, working all day with my mind off somewhere, and then at evening I would watch the pasture slope. At last, they would come in smelling of fish and woodsmoke and rotten fishing worms. Standing in the lamplit kitchen, they would pour their shining loads out into Mama's big dishpans: silver cataracts; silver-sided, orange-bellied, red-speckled trout that G.D. called the "speckled beauties," brook trout, wild and salted—a hundred or a hundred and fifty of them—like a mountain stream. After supper, out on the porch, they told of the big one Uncle Dock lost in the Red Hole; of the great fishing they had found on Cranberry; or of the flock of turkeys flushed out at Barlow Top.

When it all changed, it was not suddenly. There was no sudden summer or sudden fall; but gradually, as the years moved by, the song turned sour as the north fork of Cranberry River turned muddy. It had already begun in the 1880s, when the white pine had been cut and sent down the Greenbrier River. When the white pine loggers had come, they had brought the river-driving French Canucks. The log chutes on the skid trail glittered with ice, and they were greased with black-strap oil; the great logs roared down the chutes to the crick side. G.D. and Uncle Dock told that on a clear day when the logs were running, you could hear their heavy, screeching roar fifteen miles down river. And down at the cricks, where the loggers built their splash dams, the white pine logs splashed and swirled into the river on their way to the Ronceverte Mill.

Then there was big money in the county, and plenty of quick talk. Up at town, brick-

and-brownstone houses were built; hardware stores and whiskey stills flourished; and boardwalks were laid down. But our Over the Mountain was hardwood country, and hardwood floats too heavy. And Uncle Dock insisted, "By God, they can't take her. She's too big for them."

Hardwood *can* go out by log train; and before 1900, the railroad came, and the Italians came to build it through the steep river-cuts. They camped in shanties all along the river, and G.D. told of the shanty down on Buckley's farm that was blown to bits one night, hardly a shred of flesh left. When he went down the next morning, he found a little embroidered wool bag in bright reds, blues, and yellows, hanging up in a tree. Inside it was a woman's and a child's picture, and G.D. brought it home and kept it down in a trunk.

The day of the First Train, October 26, 1900, there was a big "speaking" up at town as the great locomotive came screaming up the valley, and the men from the railroad gave an ox roast with all the bankers, storekeepers, and lumber kings. Soon the narrow-gauge railroad began to creep up the Williams, and then its branches stretched up Tea Crick, Mountain Lick, and all the little feeder streams; and it began to carry the hardwood out.

97

Still, through most of the years of my
childhood, G.D., Uncle Dock, Cousin Rush,
and Ward went Over the Mountain and
brought home sacks of salted brook trout to
pour into Mama's big pans. The change
came slowly, and slowly a deep lament began
to run through their stories: for the muddy,
silted streams; the forest fires; the skid roads
bleeding down the eroded hills; and the
terrible waste of it all. When the jackleg
lumber companies went bankrupt, the lumber shanties were abandoned, and the rust-
ing, twisted rails. The trout began to die
with sawdust in their gills, and the great
ravaged trees were left rotting along the
ridges' slopes.

All of us along Swago Crick were tainted
by the lumber boom. Back in the 1880s, a
lot of our kinfolks, uncles and cousins, had
gone into the white pine business as rafts-
men and teamsters. And Captain Jim had
had to sell his Woodland Up-the-Hollow to
the loggers. In the early 1900s, when the
sawmill shanty town was built over on the
Buckley Flatts, G.D. went to work for them
as a bookkeeper because he needed the
money to piece out his farming and teaching school. At last, Uncle Dan'l had to sell
his dying chestnut orchard to the lumber
companies.

But the men would still go Over the Moun-

tain, persisting in it, as though the change
had not come, as though they had to find it
was not true. They would come home early,
bringing only a few fish in their haversacks,
and every time with new dark chords to
add to their lament: even on the Mountain
Lick, they would tell; even on Tea Crick
there were scars; and ravage on Black Mountain Run.

Uncle Dock died before the Great Fire of
1930, and G.D. told how the last laugh Uncle
Dock ever laughed was when he raised up
on his pillow and remembered a time, long
back, when he had taken G.D. as a little
boy Over the Mountain to fish. He told
how G.D. had caught a big one, got tangled
up in the fish and fishline, and had fallen
head first into the pool. After Uncle Dock
died, G.D. was withdrawn and silent, and
he smoked his pipe cold. But he still went
Over the Mountain, often going alone and
coming back the same day, until one summer he stopped going and never went again.

The Great Forest Fire of 1930 raged from
the headwaters of Gauley to Panther Crick
and then swept up the valley and almost
over the Elk. All week down at the village,
a smoke pall hung over the schoolyard,
and our cow spring up the hollow tasted of
smoke. In the wind that fed it, the black,
charred leaf-scraps sifted down over our

fields and pastures. After the rains came, Ward and Jess went over and walked it, all day through the black and ashes. They saw the roots of the great stumps sticking up three feet above the burned out topsoil as though they still tried to clutch the earth.

It was after the Great Fire that G.D. began to refer to Over the Mountain as The Bonnie. When G.D. was dead and Ward was the old one, Ward said that there was no place called The Bonnie, that the real name of it was Bannock Run, and that it was named for a Scotch pancake. But I know that G.D. did call it The Bonnie along at the last, and he even referred sometimes to Bonnie River. Slowly, as G.D. grew older, some several years after I was married, he began to tell my husband how it all had been: the long pavilions of shade, the clear rolling rivers, the old trails and starry camps. One night, G.D. stopped suddenly in the middle of a sentence and left it hanging there. He never mentioned Over Bonnie again. Instead, he sat in his chair by his old Sea Chest and told me and my husband about the sea: the day they moved through Magellan Straits, or the night of the great storm out on the Pacific; and Over Bonnie was, for G.D., just as though it had never been.

But for me, the lumber companies had

not cut The Bonnie, nor the Great Fire
burned it to blackened claws. Because I was
born a woman and had not gone, *could* not
go, it lay for me as I had first found it as a
girl-child by the winter fireplace, listening
to the men's wonder tales. In my obsession
and possession, the hunter men still walked.
The great trees lifted forever across my vi-
sion, and the sounding waters still ran. My
dream of the American forest was deep and
mystic and old; but the dream itself was
always in the distance, moving before the
seekers like the sun.

The Coming of the Roads

The chestnut blight came slowly, a gray
quiet death. At first there was a canker on
one old tree, and then the canker spread.
The spores blew in wind, and the branches
began dying.

We had always called Uncle Dan'l's trees
"the chestnut orchard," just across our line
fence on the flat knoll of his part of Old
Tom's farm. Forty or fifty big American
chestnut trees stood there together, as the
old men had saved them from the first clear-
ings back in Indian times, and for generations they had been the neighborhood nut-
ting ground. On crisp autumn days, the
hilltop would be full of chestnut pickers
scattering the yellow leaves with their sticks
and picking up the sweet, brown, silver-
tailed nuts. As we moved along under the
trees, the leaves rustled, the bluejays cawed,
and the sweet smell of autumn dust rose
around us. When we stopped to listen, we
could hear the squirrels chattering up in

the branches and the chestnuts falling like slow rain.

When Uncle Dan'l sold his orchard to the lumber company, the lumberjacks came in and cut it down, and then our four trees over on the home place cankered and died. In a few years, gray ghosts of the chestnut trees stood against the skyline, their bark all sloughed off. All across the mountains their bare arms reached up to the sky, and down below the new road came and began to tie our Swago Farm to the world.

When the new road was finished, it was hard, smooth, and gray-colored, and the Model T's came chugging along it, and the fancy Chevrolets, Maxwells, and Jewetts. When you went in by horse or foot, you could live almost anywhere, and the whole Swago mountain country had been scattered with wilderness farms, houses, and old one-room schools. But after the road was finished, new houses and new schoolhouses were built alongside it, and then the barns came down too. Then the gas stations came, and the little Dew Drop Inns. Back in the hills, the old houses and schoolhouses rotted down, blackberry vines crept over the broken porches, and the eyeless windows stared out at the encroaching wilderness.

Once G.D. got his own Model T, he had so much trouble getting it in through the swamp muck and the drifted snow that we too built our new house and moved over to the road. G.D. carried part of the old house with us: Captain Jim's two stone chimneys and his black walnut fireboard. After we moved and had clean running water and French doors and a breakfast nook, G.D. never went back to the old house that still stood under the hill and had been turned into a hay barn. It was almost as though Granny Fanny had jerked her thorn broom handle out of the world's axis and the whole contraption began to rattle and whirl. We three older kids began going off to college, and I began to publish poems and went dancing with Louis Untermeyer.

G.D. and Mama had planned to support all four of us children through at least two years of college, and then to let us make our own way by teaching school, saving our money, and going to summer terms. Ward and Elizabeth went first, and then I went with Elizabeth to the university as a freshman when I was sixteen years old. I had one year there, but I spent so much money that G.D. jerked me out as soon as I had a certificate and let me make my own way from there on in.

105

Sometime in the fall of my sixteenth year, I composed my first poem, working on a borrowed typewriter in my dormitory room. Though I had no boyfriend, it was a poem of love and passion: "When scarlet clouds fly by the moon, I'm always in my memories with you." I read the poem to myself and something happened to me. I had felt such joy in the writing itself and in the rhythms of the lines that I swore a vow that I would be a poet and write poems forever.

Soon after, in one of the old soon-to-be-abandoned schoolhouses, I taught my first school. It was the winter of 1930, just before the yellow school buses started running. We always called it the School up in the Brush Country, but its official name was Pleasant Hill. The schoolhouse stood on an eroded hilltop and had two decaying privies hidden out in the brush. I walked in three and a half miles each way, or boarded around with the families and walked with the Wilfong children up Ress Wilfong's hollow to the schoolhouse hill.

The schoolhouse stood on posts, and the sheep that pastured in the schoolyard sheltered under the floor. Sometimes, in the middle of a class, we could hear them bumping around under us, bawling. We had a flagpole and flag, a stove, desks, a bench, a water cooler, one shelf of worn-out books,

and hooks on the wall to hang our over-
coats; but in the winter of 1930, we didn't
hang our coats much, for the board of education had no money to fix the broken window sash. I tried to fix it with rags, and I
kept the fire boomed up, but the blizzard
winds came howling in. I taught most of
that winter in my warm leather jacket with
a red tam-o'-shanter on my head.

I had twenty-six pupils in all eight grades,
and though I had studied "educational meth-
ods" in college, I had learned nothing about
teaching school. So I remembered Miss
Anne Correll and called the kids, one class
at a time, up to the Recitation Bench. At
noon we gathered around the stove, and
the kids ate their white beans and jelly-
bread sandwiches. Everybody had apples,
and there were still a few wild American
chestnuts and plenty of fall blackberries
and wild goose plums. Often at night we
would go from house to house, eating homegrown popcorn and apples and playing our
mountain music: "The Little Mowhee,"
"Wildwood Flower," and "Red Wing."

The door peg and Granny's broom handle
had held the world, but by 1932 Granny
lay bed-sick over at Aunt Mat's and everybody was talking about the hard times. The
Great Depression was reaching its low point.

There were stores going out of business and a lot of men walking the road. Then the government started giving away "commodities," and Miss Moss Miller brought Mama a whole poke full of stuff: big grapefruit and lard and canned beef. There were foreclosures: Uncle Hunter's drug store failed, and he had to go to work on the county roads with a pick and shovel. Then the bank took Uncle Dan'l's farm; and one winter morning, Uncle Dan'l died of pneumonia, from walking his line fences in the snow.

Sometime during the Depression, Wint's store burned down, and nobody knew why. The store went up like a box of tinder, and all over the neighborhood the eerie light shivered in the sky. When the fire got to the shelf of shotgun shells, the shells exploded and shot off, whizzing into the night like Roman candles. All the store goods, and all the men's tall tales, and our village center went up that night in a great display of fireworks, a kind of blazing last gesture of defiance against the coming of Franklin Delano Roosevelt and his alphabet soup.

The very night of the day we moved over to the road, Granny Fanny died. She had been in bed over at Aunt Mat's for nearly a year, sometimes sitting up against the pillow knitting socks. I had been over to see

her a few weeks before and had told her
about the new calves and how the garden
was planted, and on my way back across
the pasture that evening I had felt the strange
hovering in the air of death's gray wing.

The undertaker put Granny Fanny into
a fine black dress with white ruffles at her
wrists and throat. Everybody said how she
looked so "natural," but she didn't look
natural to me. She looked more like some
fine, proud mountain queen who had ruled
over all her people and had never bruted or
slaved. I was a grown girl by then and had
gone off to college, and I had made my vow
to be a poet and learned all hundred verses
of Omar Khayyam's *Rubaiyat* by heart. When
they took Granny Fanny up to our grave-
hill in the black hearse, I went to her in my
new white silk dress, carrying an armful of
red poppies, for I had read in the decadent
fin de siècle poetry of Algernon Charles Swin-
burne that poppies are for sleep:

Thou art more than the day or the morrow,
    the seasons that laugh or that weep;
For these give joy and sorrow; But thou,
    Proserpina, sleep.

During the years of my brush country
schoolteaching, I would go out into the
woodland or sit under my oil lamp in my

bathrobe in my unheated room at Oley
Jackson's log house, and write lyric poems.
Soon, I began to send poems out, copying
them crookedly on G.D.'s typewriter; I published one in *Stardust*, a then current little
poetry magazine, and one in the *Columbus
Dispatch*. I found an advertisement for another little poetry magazine, *Kaleidoscope*,
in Dallas, Texas, and I submitted a thin
manuscript to a prize contest they had. The
prize was publication of a hundred copies of
a little book of poems, and I won it; so in
1931, *Mountain White* was published, with
its dying lover poems, its stoic mountaineer
poems, its clever Dorothy Parker poems, and
two or three good poems in my own style.

I kept writing, teaching, and going back
to college, until I finally managed to gradu-
ate from the teachers' college down at Athens
when I was twenty-five years old. I had a
degree in English, though I knew not a whit
of grammar beyond the noun and the verb.
But a magnetic professor there, S. L. Mc-
Graw, had helped me to discover the world
of books and philosophical thought. I settled
down, worked hard, and lived an almost in-
spired life that next year, in the company of
William Thorndike, William James, and Paul
Elmer More, as I taught the home school
in the Swago village and lived at home on
the farm.

I kept my vow to myself and continued
to write poems. I sent them off to the magazines and, mostly, I got them back. One
day, in exchange for my poem "Song in the
Saddle," a check came from *Forum* magazine up in New York. As I walked home up
through Uncle Dan'l's pasture, the weeds
were purest gold and I ran to the yard gate
to tell Mama. Later I won a prize of twenty-
five dollars, got into *Social Science,* and by
the fall of 1936, I had begun to sell poems to
the *American Mercury* where Louis Untermeyer was the editor. Mr. Untermeyer wrote
me letters of encouragement and praise for
several months, and then he wrote that he
would be speaking at our state teachers'
convention in Huntington and asked if I
planned to attend.

I went on the C. and O. train in my best
wool dress and my black rabbit fur coat
from Sears Roebuck, rode down the Greenbrier division on through Charleston and
got myself registered at the Pritchard Hotel.
On Friday morning, I met Mr. Untermeyer
for a poetry session, and he kept three poems
to take back to New York. Just as I was
leaving, he asked if he could escort me to
the formal dance that evening. I had nothing appropriate to wear, but he insisted
and, finally, I agreed.

When I got back to my hotel, there was

111

a message for me to call my Cousin Pearl.
Cousin Pearl had been born in a mountain
cabin, but now she was married to a rich
lawyer with a big house in Huntington, and
she had a daughter about my age, Cousin
Ann. Cousin Pearl wanted me for dinner
that evening, and as we sat at her fine table
talking about our kinfolks, I mentioned my
date with Mr. Untermeyer. Cousin Pearl
and Cousin Ann rushed me upstairs to
Ann's closet, dressed me in flowing white
satin, a velvet cape of purest turquoise, turquoise earrings and slippers, powdered me
and painted me, and thrust a gold mesh
evening purse into my hand. They put me
into a taxi, and I rode through the streets of
Huntington in a misty turquoise dream.

Though I could not dance, Mr. Untermeyer labored my big-boned peasant body
carefully around the ballroom floor, and
told me his joke about the three little don-
keys: Don Quixote, *danke schön*, and the
other "donkey" I can never remember. Now,
I remember little really — only the golden
music and pearly lights and what seemed to
me the utter glamor, a million miles from
my dusty schoolroom and feeding the cows
off of the winter haystacks.

Then I was back in my room, my face
misted in the mirror. I stood there a mo-
ment, and then took Cousin Ann's clothes

off, wrapped them up to return them, and after the next day's teachers' meetings, I took the Greenbrier train back to the Swago Farm.

I lived on the farm and taught school all that winter, and in the summer of 1937, I began my own journey over the mountain to Oxford, Ohio, to work on a master's degree. I requested that I be allowed to do my thesis in creative writing, a book of poems, and I gave my adviser, Walter Havighurst, an outline of a fictional mountain land called Gauley, its history from the pioneers to the lumberjacks and the new coal mines and macadam roads. That fall, I went back to teach the home school and wrote a hundred poems for a book called *Gauley Mountain*.

In 1938, I went back for the second semester at Miami of Ohio and won the Atlantic Monthly Poetry Prize. The success, or maybe the exhaustion, must have gone to my head, because I did the most stupid of the three most stupid things I have done in my life: I married, and the marriage lasted three weeks. The divorce cost me thirty-five dollars, but it seems to me now a no-fault divorce, and one that left only temporary scars. We wished each other happy landing, and I went off to a dark, dazed winter at the University of Iowa Writers' Workshop. I met Archibald MacLeish there that winter, and he took my *Gauley Mountain* manuscript off to New York where it was published by Harcourt Brace in 1939.

In the summer of 1938, at the Bread Loaf Writers' Workshop, I had met Roger Pease, a hard-headed, earth-loving Yankee schoolmaster, and we had quarreled in Robert Frost's poetry class. Roger and I were married in the summer of 1939 and we began our wandering through all the years of the Second World War.

I left the Swago Farm in the summer of 1939 and never went back again except as a visitor. Before I left, I dug up some iris roots over at the old house and took them with me. I planted them beside a red barn in the Berkshires of Massachusetts, where Roger and I went to live.

Night at the Commodore

After I left the farm, I often felt as I had when I used to plumb the depth of water as a child. In summer, after every big rainstorm, a flood would come, and our tiny cow-spring trickle would become a roaring stream that flowed foamy and green over the leaning grasses. I would go out barefoot in the early morning with a long straight pole; and with my dress tied up above my knees I would wade along the shallows to measure the deep holes. I felt my way out into the current and walked slowly upstream, my feet and legs stinging with the cold. As I walked on and on up through the wild morning, I would become John Ridd of *Lorna Doone* with his trident, walking up the spate of Doone Valley. Then the mountains would come dark and close around me. I walked until I could feel the black danger and death in it. As I am walking still. For you walk to death, don't you? Because you cannot ride.

Aunt Malindy told me that old women

in the night can see; and now that I am old
and often cannot sleep at night, I see pictures in the dark. I close my eyes and long-
ago pictures float before me, all in color and
shadow, framed in the soft fog of the years.
Most often, I seem to be standing in our
yard at home and looking in through the
"big room" window, and we are all there together in the firelight. G.D., my brother
Ward, Uncle Dock, and Cousin Rush are
by the fireplace spitting and smoking and
talking about Over the Mountain; and I am
there myself, listening. Farther back from
the fire, Mama is peeling apples; Granny
Fanny is winding her hanks of wool, and
her old gargoyle clock is ticking. Elizabeth
is holding Little Jim on her lap, and Aunt
Malindy sits in the rocker in her fat black
sateen dress, her hands folded in perfect
content. Up above us, the picture of Captain Jim hangs on the wall.

I can see all this before me in the night,
and then it fades away and I see my brother
Young Jim, now sixty-nine years old, still
farming our land, sowing lime by helicopter
over Bridger's Gap. Or I see Blix, Jim's and
Annabelle's son; and then Blix's only son,
Little Jamie, nine years old, who sometimes
helps his grandfather turn out the coral rocks
or wrestle big bales of hay up into the barn
that was once our faded cottage. Sometimes

I see my hepatica rock, with the walking
fern and maidenhair; or my white calf named
Lily. Sometimes I can see Clarence Smith,
our funeral director, looking down at G.D.'s
grave and saying, "Many a lame dog did
this man help over the stile." Then, and
quite suddenly, I may see a dying soldier in
my picture; and there is blood and mud
and death.

These days I see the war pictures more
and more: the mixed up pictures from the
Second World War, which was *my* war more
than any of the others I have lived through.
Often I see Howard Wilfong from my 1930
one-room school. Howard is in the control
tower of his ship, the *U.S.S. Borie*, when
suddenly a Jap kamikaze plane screams down
and takes the tower. Old women in the
night can see. Some nights I cannot sleep
at all.

When I left the farm, it seemed that suddenly, or *almost* suddenly, I was out in the
world. Roger and I were married and travel-
ing the old trains hooting through the pass:
the C. and O.'s Sportsman and Fast Flying Virginian; the Silver Rocket hurtling
through the prairie night; the Southern
through the piney woods of Georgia; the
old sit-up-all-night Pacemaker roaring west
to Chicago. All at once I was buying my

117

suits at Lord and Taylor's; and I, still in my Sears Roebuck shoes! On one of these wandering train rides, Roger and I and our baby, Doug, came one early September to visit with G.D. and Mama on the farm.

We were all sitting on the front porch that night: G.D. and Mama, Rog and I, my brother Jim, and our old collie herd dog lying at Jim's feet. We were sitting and talking, or not talking; and it was a still, crisp, fragrant night. The clover meadow was in new stubble, the wisteria shadows falling over the porch swing; and down under the wisteria, the crickets were crying their "six weeks till frost." Then the collie got up, whining a little. He turned around backward and looked down at his bed. A strange pale light began moving in over the porch railing. Suddenly we all saw a faint glow quivering in the sky over Bridger's Gap: the Northern Lights!

We ran out into the yard and looked up over us. The whole round of the heavens was beginning to quiver with a wild, flickering crown. At first from the north; then the east and south and west joined; and the green-red-blue-gold-purple spear tent was streaming up to the point of the heavens and riving as it came: the great crown borealis of September 1941.

As I stood there, a kind of awe and fear

came to me, as though God had not yet un-
loosed His might. But He had it, held back
somewhere in the banked fire of the Worlds.
The borealis began to fade and die down,
and we went back to the porch. The blue
September fog spread across the meadows.
We sat there in the quiet darkness, September 8, 1941, just three months before Pearl
Harbor.

Roger and I spent the years of the war
teaching at the rich boys' prep school in
Aiken, South Carolina. I planted my iris
roots from the farm again, this time in front
of a faculty cottage. Doug was a year old in
October 1941 and just beginning to talk.
One of his first words was "airplane," for
the bombers flew everyday over the school
playing field in black formation. The war
leaped and swirled around us in a kind of
controlled madness; or it dragged on and
on in an eternity of waiting, like water drip-
ping from a roof edge.

Now the time is only a cry and a shuffle
of mixed-up names: Bataan Death March,
Burma Road, Java Sea; and the *Lexington*,
FDR, Adolph Hitler, cattle cars, Guadalcanal, gas station, Savo Island, Iwo Jima,
ration cards, Gabriel Heater, Betty Grable,
Casablanca, Anzio Beach. The news came
from home that Cousin Bill had gone with

119

Patton, and Cousin Buck went down over
the English Channel. Double cousin J.B.
was in the 82nd Airborne—Salerno, Nor-
mandy, wounded in the Battle of the Bulge.
Then, after the war, "Red" Jeffries, from up
the Crick, came home from Bataan and sat
in J.B.'s filling station drinking pop. Finally
we learned the date on which Howard Wilfong died: August 12, 1945—three days after
peace was declared.

It's been more than forty years now since
the night at the Commodore Hotel, but it
still comes back to me out of the shadows
and will not stop. It is still as clear as it was
in its own stabbing hour. I forget where we
had been or where we were going that hot
August night, but Rog and Doug and I were
getting off a train in Grand Central Station. Long, long before, there had been Old
Tom's bison coming down to the salt lick in
the twilight; and now I was taking a yellow
taxi to the Commodore Hotel.

As soon as we were registered, Rog went
off on some errand. I took Doug and an
evening paper and went to our room. I gave
Doug a quick bath and stuffed him into
bed. Then, relaxing over a cigarette and a
glass of water, I sat down to read the evening news. When I looked at the headlines,
I saw a word, a phrase, that I had never

seen before. It was big and black, leaping out at me from the front page, and it was spelled A-T-O-M-I-C B-O-M-B.

August 6 and 7, 1945: the news story about a place called Hiroshima, a mushroom cloud uprisen, a triumph, burning flesh. I sat there staring down at the black newsprint, and something tore loose in my soul. Then, as from some far leafy distance, I saw Old Tom and George Rogers Clark wading the frozen swamps of the Wabash. So it was all for this? The blood on the snow at Valley Forge, on the sands of Guadalcanal? All for this that old Tim McCarty, because he knew "the hard price of Freedom," gave his sons? "Daniel, Preston, Justin, James, Thomas."

I got up and walked slowly over to the window where the lights of the neon towers were piercing across the north. Then it came to me, there above the roaring traffic and strange light of this strange city. It came to me, in the old superstitions of us mountain people, like a fireball in the night, a Death Omen. Aunt Malindy had seen hers in the sky over Buckley Mountain the night her brother Potts had been killed at Gettysburg; now mine over Hiroshima and over the Commodore Hotel. Only mine wasn't about Brother Potts. It was more about the human race, and more than that, about Earth itself.

121

That was the night the world changed. It wasn't joy that died, or faith, or resolution; for all these come back. It was something else, something deep and earth-given that died that night in the Commodore. Never again would I be able to say with such infinite certainty that the earth would always green in the springtime, and the purple hepaticas come to bloom on my woodland rock. For these, the earth and its seasons, had always been my certainty—going beyond death, beyond the death of all my people, even beyond the death of the farm; the sun in the morning, the darkness at night, the certain roll of the seasons, the "old blue misties" sweeping out of the north.

About the Author

LOUISE MCNEILL *was born in West Vir-*
ginia in 1911 on the farm where her family
has lived since 1769. Her first major collec-
tion of poems, *Gauley Mountain*, was published by Harcourt Brace in 1939 with a
foreword by Stephen Vincent Benet. She
is the author of four other collections of
poems, including *Paradox Hill* (1972) and
Elderberry Flood (1979). Ms. McNeill's poetry
has been published in *The Atlantic Monthly*,
Harper's, *Poetry*, *The Saturday Review*, and
many other magazines and anthologies.
She has also published fiction in *The Farm
Journal*, and essays in *Northwest Review* and
Appalachian Heritage. Ms. McNeill taught
for thirty-five years until her retirement
in 1972.

Among Ms. McNeill's honors are the
Atlantic Monthly Poetry Prize and the
annual book award of the West Virginia
Library Association. She has been Poet
Laureate of West Virginia since 1977 and

in 1985 was named West Virginian of the year. In 1988 she received the Appalachian Gold Medallion from the University of Charleston, West Virginia. She and her husband, Roger Pease, live with their son, Douglas and his wife Rae, in South Windsor, Connecticut.